SELF-TRUST

*A Study of Reason, Knowledge
and Autonomy*

KEITH LEHRER

CLARENDON PRESS · OXFORD
1997

Oxford University Press, Walton Street, Oxford OX2 6DP

Oxford New York
Athens Auckland Bangkok Bogota Bombay
Buenos Aires Calcutta Cape Town Dar es Salaam
Delhi Florence Hong Kong Istanbul Karachi
Kuala Lumpur Madras Madrid Melbourne
Mexico City Nairobi Paris Singapore
Taipei Tokyo Toronto

and associated companies in
Berlin Ibadan

Oxford is a trade mark of Oxford University Press

Published in the United States by
Oxford University Press, Inc., New York

British Library Cataloguing in Publication Data
Data available

Library of Congress Cataloging-in-Publication Data
Lehrer, Keith
Self-trust: a study of reason, knowledge, and autonomy / by Keith Lehrer.
Includes bibliographical references (p.).
ISBN 0-19-823665-4
ISBN 0-19-823694-8 (Pbk.)
1. Philosophy of mind. 2. Man. 3. Self (Philosophy) I. Title.
B945.L4453S45 1996 128—dc20 96–21872

Typeset by Invisible Ink
Printed in Great Britain by
Biddles Ltd, Guildford and King's Lynn

To all my students
Who make it all worthwhile
In Tucson, Graz, and everywhere

PREFACE

This book was thought about over a lifetime and written over a short time. I wrote it for my students in a seminar I taught in the autumn of 1994, forty years after I first discovered philosophy in a class from Juarez Paz, a brilliant teaching assistant, at the University of Minnesota. It is a very personal document. It claims to be about many things but is really only about me. My apologies. You have been warned. Please forgive the strangeness of my scholarship. I have appended some footnotes, and references at the end of chapters, to give some credit where credit is remembered due. I have learned so much from so many that I have quite forgotten from whom I learned what. I know that my teachers, Wilfrid Sellars, who is sadly gone, and Roderick Chisholm, who is happily yet with us, are responsible for much that is contained herein, but so is Thomas Reid, who became a mentor of mine nearly two centuries after his death. He died in 1796, and this book, appearing at the end of 1996, closes a loop between me and him and is intended as a celebration of his life. I have read a good deal, listened even more, and thought about philosophy all the time. I am not sure whether anything good has come of it or not, but whatever has come of it, whether good or bad, clever or foolish, clear or obscure, deep or shallow, is here. And that is all that I have to say about this by way of introduction except to apologize for the scholarship. I encourage all who read this book to ennoble themselves by the search for truth rather than by the citation of references, even if, in so doing, they cite me not. I forgive them their neglect in advance and ask forgiveness of them. It is the quest for truth that ennobles us and all we do, not the keeping of records which, anyway, has become impossible. But do let me know what I should read. I am not done yet.

All of the material contained herein was written or rewritten for this volume. The philosophical content of the book overlaps with some published and forthcoming work in a variety of ways. Some of the chapters overlap in wording as well as content, and they are listed below. All such material was rewritten for this volume, however, and the conclusions sometimes differ from those contained in the other work. The overlap is as follows:

Chapter 3. This is a modification of my essay, 'Supervenience, Coherence and Trustworthiness', published in Elias E. Savelos and Umit D. Yalcin (eds.), *Supervenience: New Essays*. Copyright Cambridge University Press, 1996.

Chapter 4. This chapter contains material from two essays, 'Metamental Ascent: Beyond Belief and Desire', my presidential address published in the *Proceedings and Addresses of the American Philosophical Association*, vol. 63, No. 3 (1986), and 'Love and Autonomy', in Roger Lamb (ed.), *Love Analyzed*. Copyright © 1996 by Westview Press. Reprinted by permission of Westview Press.

Chapter 5. This chapter also contains material from 'Love and Autonomy'.

Chapter 7. This chapter contains material from 'Skepticism, Lucid Content, and the Metamental Loop', in Andy Clark, Jesus Ezquerro, and Jesus M. Larrazabel (eds.), *Philosophy and Cognitive Science: Categories, Consciousness and Reasoning* (Kluwer Academic Publishers, 1996).

I gratefully acknowledge the permissions granted by the presses who first published my articles to use the materials for this book.

I conclude with my thanks to my assistants, Linda Radzik, Jennifer Ryan, and Joel Pust, who helped me to improve the manuscript in many ways and earned my gratitude for their labours and their insightful philosophical criticism. I began writing the book in Paris while an

Associate of CREA (Centre de Recherche en Epistémologie Appliquée, École Polytechnique, Paris), and continued while part of a group supported by a grant from the National Endowment for the Humanities, and wish to thank both for their support. I put in the final touches while a Visiting Fellow at the School for Advanced Study and Birkbeck College, University of London.

Keith Lehrer
27 March 1996

CONTENTS

A keystone loop in the ceiling of the chapel at Estavayer, Switzerla

Self-Trust and the Loop of Reason

Most books contain theories, and so does this one. But this book is also a picture and a hope. It is a book about reason, love, knowledge, wisdom, autonomy, and consensus. There are three unifying ideas which tie these matters together. The first is the idea that what is uniquely human is the capacity for metamental ascent, the capacity to consider and evaluate first-order mental states that arise naturally within us. The second is that such evaluation is based on a background system, on an evaluation system, and positive evaluation yields acceptance or preference concerning the object of the first-order states of belief and desire. The evaluation of beliefs and desires is essential to reason and love, knowledge and wisdom, autonomy and consensus.

A primary function of metamental ascent and higher-order evaluation is the resolution of personal and interpersonal conflict. Evaluation implies value. When we evaluate, we determine the worth, merit, value of things on the basis of an evaluation system. Metamental ascent and higher-order evaluation depend on our ability to compare the worth of things, to decide what is more worthy of our trust and what is less worthy of our trust. The third unifying idea concerns states that loop together the states within the system and structure of evaluation. These states are not the foundations of evaluations, nor are they the final stage of evaluation; they are the keystones of evaluation which hold the structure together with a loop which is itself supported by the things it holds together. The keystone loops the mind together. To choose another metaphor, it is a fixed point vector of the brain that unifies a neural assembly.

Metamental ascent transcends the mind to reach the metamind and loops back onto the body.

My picture is of a building of arches such as the chapel
at Estavayer, Switzerland; a chapel of the mind, held together at the top with a keystone loop. This is a picture of
the individual mind but also of the social mind. The individual and society are unified by a loop of metamental ascent and descent tying mind and nature together into one
unified system.

Reason and Evaluation

Let us begin with reason. Reason has had a bad press from
time to time. Romantics, existentialists, feminists, to men-
tion but a few, have complained that reason forces conformity to alleged universal rules upon the individual. Such
alleged rules, it is averred, may represent the attempt to
force social conformity and limit individual autonomy. I
wish to propose a conception of reason grounded upon
self-trust and individual evaluation of social norms. I will
argue, eventually, that consensus is based on the aggregation of individual evaluation, just as individual evaluation
is based on the aggregated consensus of the group. I will
offer a model of aggregation to explain how. I begin with
the individual, conceding the social influence of thought
and evaluation, because all individuals, however shaped
and formed by others, must also decide for themselves
what they accept and prefer.

Whether the individual is reasonable in what he or she
thus accepts and prefers, depends on whether he or she is
worthy of his or her own trust in this respect. This remark,
if you agree with it, will lead you in a new direction concerning your conception of the life of reason. The acceptance of some rule and preference for conformity to it may
make you worthy of the trust of another and make it, consequently, reasonable for that person to accept or prefer the
conclusions you draw, but, if you are completely ignorant
of the merits of the rule, you may not be worthy of your

own trust, and, consequently, the conclusions you draw may not be reasonable ones for you to accept or prefer. Another may, of course, inform you of the merits of the rule and what you conclude, but you must decide whether the other is worthy of your trust in order to be reasonable in accepting or preferring what you do in fact accept or prefer. To decide that, you must be worthy of your trust as you evaluate the other. Your reasonableness and your life of reason depend on whether you are worthy of your own trust.

Beyond Belief and Desire to Acceptance and Preference

There are many things that I believe or desire that are not worthy of my trust. Beliefs and desires often arise capriciously and sometimes perversely within me and contrary to my better judgement. I am not in a position to say that all my beliefs and desires are worthy of my trust. But what makes me worthy of my trust is my capacity to evaluate my beliefs and desires, and that is the role of metamental ascent. That is transcendence to a life of reason. This is not a deprecation of feeling, belief, and desire, for they supply us with information to evaluate and are essential to us. But they differ in their worth and constantly conflict. They are like a group of workers that present themselves for some task but must be evaluated for their skills and be organized for their efforts.

The positive evaluation of belief, I have called *acceptance*, and the positive evaluation of desire, I have called *preference*.[1] The objective of acceptance is to accept something if it is worth accepting as true and to avoid acceptance of what is not. The objective of preference is to prefer what has merit and to avoid preferring what does not. Acceptance and preference represent our best efforts to accept what has worth and prefer what has merit, and each has an important function in thought, inference, and choice. Such func-

[1] Keith Lehrer, *Theory of Knowledge* (Boulder, Colo., and London, 1990); and Keith Lehrer, *Metamind* (Oxford, 1990).

tional states are typically the positive evaluation of something believed or desired, but this is not essential to their
nature. I may consider something that I do not believe, and
evaluate it positively, producing acceptance of it. Belief
does not automatically result, though in some cases it will.
Subjects will continue to believe positive things about
themselves that they were told in an experimental setting,
even when they are told in an official debriefing that what
they were told was chosen at random and has no basis in
fact. The subjects *accept* that they have no reason to think
what they were told is true, but they seem to continue to *believe* it none the less.[2] Here belief and acceptance, the first-
level attitude and the second-level evaluation of it, separate.
Similarly, if I desire something but evaluate it negatively,
thus preferring something else, the preference will not automatically carry desire with it. Our evaluations of belief
and desire do not automatically change what we believe
and desire, somewhat to our dismay but, perhaps, in concealed ways, to our advantage.[3]

Acceptance is akin to reflective judgement, and preference to reflective decision, but they are not the same thing.
We can accept something, and reasonably so, without reflection, and we can prefer something, and reasonably so,
without reflection. There are cases in which we have background information that enables us to accept and prefer
without reflection, as when I accept that some water from
the tap will quench my thirst and prefer to drink it. Positive
evaluation may occur without reflection when reflection
would be otiose and would leave unchanged our intellectual and practical attitudes concerning what we accept or
prefer. One may think of acceptance and preference as
kinds of intellectual and practical judgement, though such
judgement need not be the product of deliberation and
ratiocination.

    [2]Richard Nisbett and Lee Ross, *Human Inference: Strategies and Short-
comings of Social Judgment* (Englewood Cliffs, N. J., 1980).
    [3] For more on these issues see Alfred Mele, 'Incontinent Believing',
Philosophical Quarterly, 36 (1986), 212–22.

Reasonableness and Self-Trust

Acceptance and preference are our best efforts to use the information we have to be reasonable. But what is required for us to succeed? Put the question another way: what is required to convert acceptance into reasonable acceptance and preference into reasonable preference? A sceptic may concede the distinction between first-order states and the higher-order evaluation of them, acceptance and preference, but deny that we are reasonable to accept what we do or reasonable to prefer what we do. What converts acceptance into reasonable acceptance and preference into reasonable preference? How are we to take the first step in the life of reason?

The life of reason begins with self-trust. Consequently, I articulate my excursion into the life of reason in the first person speaking about myself but with the intention that you will adopt the first-person pronoun as your own. I cannot reply to an external sceptic nor to the sceptic within my own head without self-trust. Suppose a sceptic within or without says to me, 'You are ignorant and foolish in all things, you know nothing and are wise in nothing. Persuade me otherwise if you can, that you are reasonable in what you accept or prefer, but be careful, as you proceed, not to appeal to anything that you accept or prefer, for that is mere ignorance or folly.' The path of reply is blocked at the very beginning, for I must appeal to what I accept as premisses, I have nothing better. So I may justly ignore the challenge of replying to the sceptic without trusting what I accept.

The first step in the life of reason is self-trust. I trust myself in what I accept and prefer, and I consider myself worthy of my trust in what I accept or prefer. Acceptance and preference are, after all, my best efforts to obtain truth and merit, and if they are not worthy of my trust, then I am not worthy of my trust, and reason is impotent. The sceptical path is sterile. Let us try the other path, the path of self-trust. This path is a simple one. I trust myself. I am worthy of my trust. I am worthy of my trust concerning what I prefer and accept. Down this path, pointed out by Thomas Reid,[4] we find an answer to the sceptic. If I am worthy of my trust concerning what I accept and prefer, I can find an argument for the reasonableness of both. That argument will lead you and me to the keystone of knowledge and wisdom.

Theoretical Reasonableness

Let me begin with intellectual or theoretical reason, reason concerning acceptance, and then turn to practical or applied reason, reason concerning preference. I will finally show you how theory and practice are joined and unified by the keystone loop. I remember Descartes and accept that I exist, Moore and accept that I see my hand before me. I believe these things, and evaluate them positively in terms of the evaluation system that I have acquired from experience and ratiocination, from weighing and reflecting. There are objections about demons and deceptions, but they are less worthy of my trust than my acceptance of these simple things. It is these simple things and not the things about demons and deceptions that I accept, because the former and not the latter are worthy of my trust. They are not the foundation of what I accept, they are but examples of what I accept. I accept something. I accept that p.

The Acceptance Argument

Here is my argument for the reasonableness of what I accept, that p, found on the path of self-trust.

(1) I accept that p.
(2) I am worthy of my trust concerning what I accept.
(3) I am worthy of my trust concerning my acceptance of p.

[4] Thomas Reid, *The Works of Thomas Reid, D.D.*, 8th edn., ed. Sir William Hamilton (Edinburgh, 1895).

But now I find myself already happily stumbling on a conclusion concerning reasonableness lying before me. For if I am worthy of my trust concerning my acceptance of p, then, since the aim of acceptance is to accept what is worth accepting as true, I am reasonable to trust my acceptance of p. So I proceed to state what lies immediately before me on the path.

(4) I am reasonable to trust my acceptance of p.

One more short step. If I am not reasonable to accept that p, then I am not reasonable to trust my acceptance of p. Conversely, of course, if I am reasonable to trust my acceptance of p, then I am reasonable to accept that p. Hence, we reach a milestone on the path of reason.

(5) I am reasonable to accept that p.

This is but a small part of the way to the goal of knowledge and wisdom. Yet the first mile is the most important, and I will linger here a bit to understand this connection between self-trust and the life of reason.

There is an objection to my argument, but not to the first premiss, because if I accept nothing the problem of the reasonableness of what I accept never arises. What about the second premiss? So far I have said I must accept the second premiss, that I am worthy of my trust concerning what I accept. This need to accept my own trustworthiness appears to be an argument from despair. Unless I accept my own trustworthiness, I cannot respond to sceptical doubt and my situation is without the remedy of reason. But what reason do I have to think I am reasonable to accept that premiss (2) is true? I could attempt to justify premiss (2) with other premisses, but I must accept my trustworthiness concerning those premisses or the argument is to no avail. For what is the point of trying to prove some conclusion from premisses I accept unless I am worthy of my trust concerning those premisses? The attempt to justify premiss (2) from other premisses leads to a regress.

Another alternative would be for me to insist that I just

am reasonable to accept premiss (2) as true without any reason or explanation. The attempt to justify premiss (2) by argument appears to lead to a regress but just to insist that I am reasonable to accept premiss (2) converts it into a kind of surd of reason, something accepted but incapable of rational explanation.

Am I trapped between the regress and the surd? No, I am not. I accept premiss (2), and consequently, premiss (2) applies to itself in the argument just given above. Let the variable p in the argument above be replaced by premiss (2), the principle of my trustworthiness itself. The conclusion of the argument is, then, that I am reasonable to accept that I am worthy of my trust concerning what I accept. The argument is as follows:

(1A) I accept that I am worthy of my trust concerning what I accept.

(2A) I am worthy of my trust concerning what I accept.

(3A) I am worthy of my trust concerning my acceptance of the premiss that I am worthy of my trust concerning what I accept.

(4A) I am reasonable to trust my acceptance of the thesis that I am worthy of my trust concerning what I accept.

(5A) I am reasonable to accept that I am worthy of my trust concerning what I accept.

Conclusion (5A) is the desired one.

Have I really avoided the surd? I have after all used premiss (2A) in the argument to reach the conclusion that I am reasonable to accept (2A). Does not that leave me with an unexplained surd as the second premiss? No, for the reasonableness of accepting my trustworthiness is not unexplained. To be sure, the argument is not a proof of the truth of the conclusion, especially not to one sceptical of the premisses, especially premiss (2A). But the argument, though not a proof that could refute a sceptic, does explain my reasonableness in accepting that I am trustworthy, for the simple reason that my trustworthiness in what I accept explains why I am trustworthy in accepting my trustworthiness. If I am worthy of my trust concerning what I accept, that explains why I am worthy of my trust concerning my acceptance of my being worthy of my trust in what I accept. That is just one of the things that I accept, and I am worthy of my trust concerning what I accept, that very thing included.

The point of the argument is the explanation of the reasonableness of accepting that I am worthy of my trust concerning what I accept, even if I cannot prove that the argument is correct. The keystone second premiss of both arguments, which I rename

(A) I am worthy of my trust concerning what I accept,

applies to the acceptance of itself. This explains my trustworthiness and reasonableness in accepting (A). Is (A) thus a kind of foundation of reasonable acceptance on which the structure of reasonable acceptance rests? No, that is the wrong metaphor. The reason is that other things that I accept support and confirm premiss (A). When I consider the other things that I accept, remembering that what I accept constitutes my best effort to accept what is worth accepting as true and avoid accepting what is not, I conclude that I am worthy of my trust in what I accept.

The Keystone Loop

I do not conclude that I am infallible or free from error in all that I accept, but I do conclude that my best efforts are worthy of my trust, as premiss (A) tells us. Of course, in appealing to the things that I accept, I am assuming that I am worthy of my trust in these matters, and, consequently, as (A) is supported by the other things I accept, so my trust in my acceptance of those things depends on premiss (A). Premiss (A) is thus not a foundation, for it is supported by the acceptance of those things whose worth depends on premiss (A). The correct figure is that of a keystone, a circular or looping keystone supporting the arches of a building.

A simple arch has a keystone in the top, the other stones lean against it, and it holds the structure in place. Now think of a building composed of arches held in place by a single circular keystone. That is the model for premiss (A), a keystone in an evaluation system of reasonable acceptance. We will see how coherence with the system of reasonable acceptance leads to knowledge and wisdom, but first let us consider the meaning of the conclusions we have reached.

I am reasonable in accepting what I do because I am worthy of my trust concerning what I accept. To some the inference is obvious, but I offer clarification to those who do not find it perspicuous. Let me consider again the original argument.

(1) I accept that p.
(2) I am worthy of my trust concerning what I accept.
(3) I am worthy of my trust concerning my acceptance of p.
(4) I am reasonable to trust my acceptance of p.
(5) I am reasonable to accept that p.

When I consider accepting something, I have two options, acceptance and non-acceptance. When I accept something, I have, in effect, raised the question, to accept or not to accept, and answered the question with a positive evaluation. The statements of the argument tell us that our positive answer to the question, our acceptance, is worthy of our trust or is reasonable.

Thus, we may reformulate the argument making the comparative character of statements explicit as follows:

(1) I accept that p.
(2C) Acceptance of what I accept is more worthy of my trust than non-acceptance.
(3C) Acceptance of p is more worthy of my trust than non-acceptance of p.
(4C) Acceptance of p is more reasonable for me to trust than non-acceptance of p.
(5C) Acceptance of p is more reasonable for me than non-acceptance of p.

The argument may be more convincing in this mode. The inference from (3C) to (5C) is perhaps more perspicuous than the inference from (3) to (5) above and illuminates the connection. If I ask myself whether acceptance is more worthy of my trust than non-acceptance, and the answer is positive, then when I ask myself whether acceptance is more reasonable than non-acceptance, the answer is again positive. One purpose of my reformulation is to clarify the inference, but another is to indicate the modesty of the ultimate conclusion. I do not claim that reasonableness of acceptance, the conclusion of the argument, provides us with the kind of justification needed to obtain knowledge or the kind of evidence we might require for scientific confirmation or legal verdicts. The conclusion concerns a modest form of intellectual reasonableness, the first mile on the path of reason, where we already encountered the keystone loop.

Practical Reasonableness

Consider practical reason. The conclusion of practical reason is preference, which is the basis of choice and action. I choose what I prefer and pursue what I choose. The object of acceptance is something propositional in form, that something is the case, but the object of preference is action, that I do something. We desire things of various sorts: ice cream, love, a cold drink, a solution to a philosophical problem, an orgasm, spiritual awakening, and a myriad of other things. A preference to satisfy these desires and pursue their satisfaction is, however, a preference that I do something, that I obtain the ice cream, that I have the cold drink, that I solve the philosophical problem, and so forth.

My preference is a preference for the satisfaction of some end, usually but not always something I desire, and the pursuit of that end. I might prefer to fulfil some odious obligation and pursue that end without any desire to do so. The end is one that I evaluate positively as having merit and, indeed, as having optimal merit among conflicting ends, allowing, of course, for ties. As I do my best to obtain what has merit and avoid what does not, I reach a positive evaluation and preference based on my background system, my evaluation system. My preference is thus my best effort, based on the information I possess, to pursue what has the most merit among my options and eschew those which have less. But are my best efforts good enough? What about the cynic who says that preferences are expressions of will and outside the life of reason? Preferences are neither wise nor foolish, neither reasonable nor unreasonable, she might add, they are a surd of the will. How can I answer her?

The Preference Argument

Self-trust and the worthiness of it provide the answer. Consider the sequence of self-trust. I trust myself. I am worthy of my trust. I am worthy of my trust concerning what I accept and prefer. There is again the argument proceeding from self-trust to the conclusion of reasonableness. Suppose now that I prefer something, that I write a book, and consider the following argument:

(1P) I prefer that p.
(2P) I am worthy of my trust concerning what I prefer.
(3P) I am worthy of my trust concerning my preference for p.
(4P) I am reasonable to trust my preference for p.
(5P) I am reasonable to prefer that p.

The argument may again be rewritten revealing the comparative character of worthiness and reasonableness, as I consider whether to prefer something or not, consider the merits of preference and non-preference of the thing in question, and decide in favour of preference on the basis of coherence with my evaluation system.

The argument then becomes:

(1P) I prefer that p.

(2CP) Preference for what I prefer is more worthy of my trust than non-preference.

(3CP) Preference for p is more worthy of my trust than non-preference for p.

(4CP) Preference for p is more reasonable for me to trust than non-preference for p.

(5CP) Preference for p is more reasonable for me than non-preference for p.

So far the parallel between the arguments for the reasonableness of preference and the reasonableness of acceptance are exact, and justificatory argument would be simple reiteration. The conclusions of the reasonableness of preference and acceptance have a matching structure, but there is also a difference between them to examine.

Consider the second premiss of the argument for the reasonableness of acceptance

(A) I am worthy of my trust concerning what I accept,

and compare this to the second premiss of the argument for the reasonableness of preference:

(P) I am worthy of my trust concerning what I prefer.

We noticed above that (A) applies to itself and explains why I am reasonable to accept it. I am reasonable to accept it because I do accept it and I am worthy of my trust concerning what I accept. The simple truth of (A) explains the reasonableness of accepting (A). I cannot, of course, prove (A) without arguing in a circle, even if I use other things I accept as premisses, but the truth of (A) explains the reasonableness of accepting (A) and avoids treating (A) as a surd of reason. May I say the same of premiss (P)? There is a difference. It is my acceptance of (A), not my preference for (P), that functions in the argument above, and, correspondingly, it is the truth of (P), and not the merit of preferring (P), that explains the reasonableness of my preferences.

Consider the argument that substitutes principle (P), the

second premiss of the argument, for the variable p in all the premisses of the argument, which is as follows:

(1P) I prefer (P).
(2P) I am worthy of my trust concerning what I prefer.
(3P) I am worthy of my trust concerning my preference for (P).
(4P) I am reasonable to trust my preference for (P).
(5P) I am reasonable to prefer (P).

The argument is sound, and the second premiss, which is (P) itself, functions to reach the conclusion as in the argument for the reasonableness of acceptance; but it is the truth of (2P) or (P) and my acceptance of the truth of it that permits me to reach the conclusion. Thus, it appears that the order of my argumentation, beginning with reasonable acceptance and proceeding to reasonable preference, exhibits a linear order on the path of reason and a priority of theoretical reason over practical reason. Follow the path a bit further, however, and the path is circular.

The Loop of Reason

To reveal the loop in the path of reason, let me return to the sequence of self-trust and retrace our steps. I trust myself. I am worthy of my trust. I am worthy of my trust concerning what I accept and prefer. But what makes me consider myself worthy of my trust? I might be inclined to say I just am, and settle for a surd, but that would be as misleading as it would be unilluminating. I accept that I am worthy of my trust because of my best efforts to be so. My preferences express those efforts, and I accept that I am worthy of my trust concerning what I accept and prefer because I prefer to be worthy of my trust and pursue that end. Consider, then, the following statements:

I accept (A).
I accept (P).

The truth of these is essential to the arguments for the reasonableness of acceptance and preference, for I must accept the second premiss of each to reach the conclusion of reasonableness. But notice that (A) and (P) must also be true, and not merely accepted, if the argument is to succeed. Thus, if I am to evaluate positively,

(A) I am worthy of my trust concerning what I accept

and

(P) I am worthy of my trust concerning what I prefer,

as things that are true, then I must have a preference for being worthy of my trust concerning what I accept and prefer.

Thus I require the following:

I prefer (A).
I prefer (P).

Without these preferences, I lack the positive evaluation of (A) and (P) that I require for the acceptance of them. My acceptance of my being worthy of my trust concerning what I accept and prefer is based on my preference for it, and my preference for it is based on my acceptance of the merit of being worthy of my trust in what I accept and prefer. My preference and acceptance concerning my trustworthiness in what I accept and prefer form a loop which is the keystone supporting the structure of reasonable acceptance and preference within my evaluation system.

Objection against Trustworthiness

In the next chapter, we will consider how the keystone states provide a defence and justification of acceptance and preference and form the basis of knowledge and wisdom. But first, the acceptance argument and the preference argument require some defence and justification themselves. Premisses (A) and (P) are controversial and require further consideration. I will discuss an objection against my use of (A) and a defence against it that would be exactly analo-

gous to an objection against my use of (P) and the defence
of it. Meeting the objection will lead us to the keystone premiss concerning reasoning itself.

Consider the acceptance argument:

(1) I accept that p.
(2) I am worthy of my trust concerning what I accept.
(3) I am worthy of my trust concerning my acceptance of
p.
(4) I am reasonable to trust my acceptance of p.
(5) I am reasonable to accept that p.

The argument from (3) to (5) has been defended above, but
the crucial and controversial step in the argument is use of
premiss (2) for the inference of (3).

Universal Generalization of Trustworthiness

It would be possible to formulate premiss (2) so that my inference of (3) is deductively valid by reformulating it as a
universal generalization as follows:

(UG2) For any p, if I accept that p, then I am worthy of
my trust concerning my acceptance of p.

There is, however, a natural objection to this principle,
namely, that I am worthy of my trust in some matters concerning some subjects, but I am not worthy of my trust or,
for that matter, of the trust of anyone else in other matters.
Passion, arrogance, and/or ignorance can lead me to accept
something when I am not in a position to evaluate what is
worth accepting as true and what is not. The objection is
that in some matters I am worthy of my trust and others
not and, therefore, (UG2) is false.

There are two ways to defend (UG2). The first is to note
that if I am aware of the fact that I cannot tell what is worth
accepting and what is not in some domain, botany in my
case, for example, then I can avoid acceptance of what is
not worth accepting as true by simply not accepting anything in that domain. Thus, the case for the defence of

(UG2) is much stronger than it at first appears to be. I may withhold positive evaluation and refrain from acceptance in domains where my capacity to evaluate is deficient. The result would be that I remain worthy of my trust concerning what I accept because I refrain from accepting things when I lack the capacity to discern whether they are worth accepting as true. I follow the dictum, 'when incompetent, accept nothing.' The remaining problem is that it seems only human for me to fail to follow the dictum now and then, and I should have to be perfect in conformity to it in order render (UG2) true.

Relativized Generalization

An alternative way of meeting the objection would be to modify (UG2) so that it is relativized to the domains in which I am worthy of my trust concerning what I accept. Thus, if ($d1$), ($d2$), and so forth to (dn), are the domains in which I am trustworthy concerning what I accept, and we wish to replace (UG2) with a premiss that will suffice to avoid the regress and the surd, we might try the following:

> (UG2D) I am worthy of my trust in what I accept concerning matters in domains ($d1$), ($d2$), and so forth through (dn), including the domain of things I accept concerning whether I am worthy of my trust in what I accept.

This premiss will suffice for the conclusion of the reasonableness of anything that I accept belonging to the domains in question. It will also suffice to explain the reasonableness of accepting itself, because it says that I am worthy of my trust concerning the things that I accept concerning whether I am worthy of my trust in what I accept.

Both (UG2) and (UG2D) have a common problem. It is that I might think that I have the capacity to distinguish what is worth accepting as true from what is not in some domain when I actually lack the capacity. Indeed, if I am unworthy of my trust concerning what I accept in some domain, I may also be unworthy of my trust concerning whether I am worthy of my trust concerning what I accept in the domain; for one way of failing to be worthy of my trust is to accept that I am worthy of my trust in some matter when I am not. In short, if I am fallible about whether I am worthy of my trust, and sometimes err about whether or not I am worthy of my trust, then I will, even if I limit my acceptance to matters in which I accept that I am worthy of my trust, accept things when I am unworthy of my trust because I mistakenly accept that I am worthy of my trust.

Does this mean that the assumption that premiss (2) is true is doomed to err, unless I am faultless in the way in which I accept what I do about whether I am worthy of my trust in what I accept? No. Premiss (2) must not be interpreted as a universal generalization. Recall that premiss (2) arose in the path of self-trust from the more general and less specific premiss, I am worthy of my trust. That assumption does not imply that I am perfect or faultless. I can be worthy of my trust without being faultless. Even the best guides err sometimes, however rarely, and yet they are worthy of our trust. So, I can be worthy of my trust, even though I err, and, more specifically, I can be worthy of my trust concerning what I accept, even though I sometimes accept something when I am not worthy of my trust in doing so. The best guide remains worthy of our trust in what she does though she errs, and I remain worthy of my trust though I err.

Trustworthiness as a Capacity

I conclude that premiss (2) is true but is not properly formulated as a universal generalization. I can err about whether I am trustworthy in accepting some specific thing, think that I am trustworthy in accepting it when I am not, which shows that I should not express my general trustworthiness concerning what I accept as a universal generalization implying that I never accept anything without being worthy of my trust in accepting it. I may have the capacity to proceed virtuously, to accept what is worth accepting and not to accept what is not, but fail to exercise that capacity in a particular case. I am in such a case not worthy of my trust in what I accept, because I fail to exercise the capacity. My trustworthiness concerning what I accept is a capacity or disposition to be worthy of my trust in what I accept only, not a guarantee of perfection. It is a capacity that I improve by correcting my errors over time.

This leaves us with a final problem, namely, the reasoning:

(1) I accept that p,
(2) I am worthy of my trust concerning what I accept,

therefore,

(3) I am worthy of my trust concerning my acceptance of p.

If premiss (2) is a universal generalization, the argument is deductively valid, but if (2) is not a universal generalization, as I now propose, then the argument is not deductively valid. It is inductive. It is, however, reasonable none the less. It is reasonable in the way in which inductive reasoning from general capacities or dispositions to the specific case is reasonable. Such reasoning is fallible and defeasible, to be sure, but it is worthy of my trust. Moreover, the reasonableness of any reasoning I make depends on my being trustworthy in how I reason.

The Reasonableness of Reasoning

Reasoning involves metamental ascent and higher-order evaluation of first-order inference, which may be automatic and dubious, to determine whether the inferences are worth drawing. The positive evaluation of drawing an inference is reasoning. The analogy between acceptance, preference, and reasoning, on the one hand, and belief, desire, and inference, on the other hand, is an exact one. We must evaluate inferences, as we evaluate beliefs and desires, to arrive by metamental ascent at something worthy of our trust. It is our reasoning, like our acceptances and preferences, that constitutes our best efforts and is worthy of our trust.

I am worthy of my trust in how I reason. The loop of self-trust tying together acceptance and preference, theoretical reason and practical reason, must include reasoning itself within the loop. Indeed, reasoning is a knot that ties the loop. It is the knot that solves the general problem of induction as well as the problem just considered. Induction is reasonable if I am worthy of my trust in how I reason. The problem of the choice of rules and principles remains, but unless I am worthy of my trust in how I reason, my efforts to defend reasoning will fail.

The Reasoning Argument

Consider the following premiss:

(R) I am worthy of my trust in how I reason.

This premiss, like premisses (A) and (P) concerning acceptance and preference, may be used to conclude that I am reasonable in how I reason, including my reasoning to (R) itself. The reasoning follows a by now familiar path:

(1R) I reason that (R).
(2R) I am worthy of my trust in how I reason.
(3R) I am worthy of my trust in reasoning that (R).
(4R) I am reasonable to trust my reasoning that (R).
(5R) I am reasonable in my reasoning that (R).

This is the keystone of reasoning. Without premiss (R) or (2R) in the loop of reason, I cannot reason that my inductive inferences are reasonable. But with the positive evaluation of inference rendering my reasoning worthy of my trust, I can reason to the conclusion that I am reasonable in how I reason inductively.

In fact, the same is true of deduction. I can err in my deductive inferences quite as well as in my inductive ones, and both require the evaluation of reason. When I reason to statement (R) from my past reasonings, both inductive and deductive, the reasonableness of the reasoning, though supported by past reasonings, depends upon the truth of (R) itself. Those reasonings support the reasoning to (R) as it supports them. Premiss (R) is itself a keystone in the loop of reason which explains the reasonableness of reasoning, both inductive and deductive, while avoiding the regress and surd.

We accept and prefer that we are trustworthy in what we accept and prefer. This creates the keystone loop. We now add the segment of reason to the keystone loop. In so doing, we make explicit an assumption in the arguments for the reasonableness of acceptance and preference. The assumption is that the reasoning from premisses to conclusion in those arguments is worthy of my trust. I reason to the conclusion that I am worthy of my trust in what I accept and prefer. I must be worthy of my trust in how I reason to sustain the conclusions.

The loop of reason widens, for I must accept that I am worthy of my trust in how I reason to reach the conclusions that I am worthy of my trust and, finally, reasonable in my acceptance, preference, and reasoning. To be worthy of my trust in my acceptance, preference, and reasoning, however, I must prefer to be worthy of my trust. Given that I accept and prefer that I am worthy of my trust in my acceptances, preferences, and reasonings, I can conclude that I am worthy of my trust in these matters by way of a reasoning process that is itself worthy of my trust.

To summarize, consider the following keystone principles:

(A) I am worthy of my trust concerning what I accept.
(P) I am worthy of my trust concerning what I prefer.
(R) I am worthy of my trust concerning how I reason.

If we add the evaluations:

> I accept (A), I accept (P), I accept (R), I prefer (A), I prefer (P), I prefer (R), I reason that (A), I reason that (P), I reason that (R),

we close the keystone loop of reason. We may begin with any of them and will be led through them all in our construction of the loop of reason out of the keystone premisses of reasonable acceptance, preference, and reasoning.

The Loop of Reason and Circular Reasoning.

In the next chapter, I will refer to a metamental loop, the loop of reason, in my analysis of knowledge and wisdom. An obvious objection to this use of a loop is that it is circular reasoning, and such reasoning proves nothing. In fact, I agree. Circular reasoning proves nothing. My intention is not to prove conclusions by circular reasoning but to explain the reasonableness and justification of what we accept and prefer in terms of a principle of our trustworthiness. The truth of the principle, that is, the reality of our trustworthiness, explains many things, including the reasonableness of accepting that we are trustworthy. This is no proof of the reasonableness of accepting that we are trustworthy or worthy of our own trust, for used as a proof, it would assume the very thing to be proved. When it comes to explanation, however, the reality of our trustworthiness does, in fact, explain the reasonableness of accepting that we are trustworthy.

So, proof cannot be circular but explanation may be. The reason is a simple and familiar one. When we come to explain things, assuming our explanations are finite, we either end with some principle which is unexplained, a kind of explanatory surd, or we come to some principle that explains not only other principles but itself as well. We must choose between the surd and the loop. The advantage of the loop is that nothing need be left unexplained. Those who seek to maximize explanation will prefer the loop, as I do, but I have no proof that anyone should seek to maximize explanation in philosophy or anywhere else. The preference for leaving nothing unexplained, and entering the loop of explanation as a result, is one I act upon in developing my philosophy. I do not pretend to offer any proof that one ought to proceed in this way. I rest content with the observation that there is no fallacy in the explanatory loop. Of that I am confident. One might not have a taste for such things, one might even be philosophically offended by them, but there is no fallacy in the taste for maximizing explanation by following the path of a loop. I shall find knowledge and wisdom within the loop in the next chapter.

FOR FURTHER READING

On Reid's reply to the sceptic:

Alston, William P., 'Thomas Reid on Epistemic Principles', *History of Philosophy Quarterly*, 2 (1985), 435–52.
Lehrer, Keith, *Thomas Reid* (New York: Routledge, 1989).

On circles in justification:

Alston, William P., 'Epistemic Circularity', *Philosophy and Phenomenological Research*, 47 (1986), 1–30.
Audi, Robert, *Belief, Justification and Knowledge* (Belmont, Calif.: Wadsworth, 1988).
Chisholm, Roderick, *Theory of Knowledge*, 3rd edn. (Englewood Cliffs, N. J.: Prentice-Hall, 1989).
Hofstadter, Douglas, *Gödel, Escher, Bach: An Eternal Golden Braid* (New York: Basic Books, 1979).
Van Cleve, James, 'Foundationalism, Epistemic Principles and the Cartesian Circle', *Philosophical Review*, 88 (1979), 55–91.

On trust:

Baier, Annette, 'Trust', in Grethe Peterson (ed.), *The Tanner Lectures on Human Values* (Salt Lake City, Utah: University of Utah Press, 1992).

Holton, Richard, 'Deciding to Trust, Coming to Believe', *Australasian Journal of Philosophy*, 72 (1994), 63–76.

On reflexivity:

Bartlett, Steven (ed.), *Reflexivity: A Source-Book in Self-Reference* (New York: Elsevier Science, 1992).
Black, Max, 'Self-Supporting Inductive Arguments', *Journal of Philosophy*, 55 (1958), 718–25.
Kordig, Carl, 'Self-Reference and Philosophy', *American Philosophical Quarterly*, 20 (1983), 207–16.
Suber, Peter, 'A Bibliography of Works on Reflexivity', in Peter Suber (ed.), *Self-Reference* (Dordrecht: Nijhoff, 1987).

On induction:

Cohen, Jonathan L., *The Probable and the Provable* (Oxford: Clarendon Press, 1977).
Feigl, Herbert, 'On the Vindication of Induction', *Philosophy of Science*, 28 (1961), 212–16.
Reichenbach, Hans, 'On the Justification of Induction', *Journal of Philosophy*, 37 (1940), 97–103.

2

Knowledge and Wisdom

I ended the last chapter with the keystone loop of acceptance, preference, and reasoning. I devote this chapter to a theory of knowledge based on that loop within an evaluation system. The keystone loop in the ceiling of the chapel at Estavayer, Switzerland, illustrates the structure (see Frontispiece). The circular keystone connects and supports two arches, which, in turn, lean against the keystone and hold it in place. You may think of one arch as the arch of preference and the other arch as the arch of acceptance. The arch of acceptance includes all my acceptances about all things, commonplace things and scientific things. The arch of preference extends to all my preferences. The circular keystone is the loop of acceptances and preferences concerning reason and trustworthiness. To conclude that I am worthy of my trust concerning what I accept and prefer, I must accept the premiss that I am worthy of my trust concerning what I accept and prefer. For that conclusion to be sound, I must prefer that I be worthy of my trust concerning what I accept and prefer. I must, of course, also be worthy of my trust in how I reason from these premisses to the conclusion, but the acceptances and preferences are the conclusions reason yields. These arches, connected by the keystone loop, constitute my evaluation system.

Evaluation

What is my evaluation system? When I look within myself to find some basis for evaluation, something that sustains the evaluations, the acceptances and preferences, what do I find that makes me worthy of my trust? There are, of course, feelings, beliefs, and desires within, but it is my evaluation of these raw materials that makes me worthy of my trust in what I accept and prefer. But what are these evaluations that make me worthy of my own trust? They are, of course, my acceptances and preferences themselves, the fruits of reasoning. There is a loop of evaluation coiled within my evaluation system, a loop of acceptances and preferences that tie the system up, that tie the system down, that tie the system together. My evaluations of what is true and what has merit are what make me worthy of my trust and lead to knowledge and wisdom. I can find no standpoint apart from my preferences and acceptances from which to evaluate what is true and what has merit, for my preferences are based on what I accept about the merit of alternatives, and my acceptances are based on what I prefer to accept to obtain truth. The only way I have of knowing what is true or meritorious is based on my acceptances and preferences.

My evaluation system is, therefore, a system of acceptances and preferences including acceptances concerning preferences and preferences concerning acceptances. This evaluation system consisting of acceptances and preferences is the basis of knowledge and wisdom. A number of philosophers have placed emphasis on a principle of conservation of belief as a basis of justification for what we believe.[1] But why is it reasonable to conserve belief just because it exists? Is this just doxastic politics of the epistemic right? I suggest that the concealed reason for conserving beliefs is that we evaluate them positively, that we consider them to be worthy of our trust. The acceptance of what we believe provides a basis for justification and knowledge rather than the conservation of belief. Acceptance and preference provide a basis for knowledge and wisdom through the trustworthiness of evaluation.

How do knowledge and wisdom result from an evaluation system? Knowledge, as I have often argued, results

---

[1] Gilbert Harman, *Change in View* (Cambridge, Mass., 1986); William Lycan, *Judgement and Justification* (New York, 1988).

from acceptance of truth justified by an evaluation system and undefeated by error.[2] Knowledge based on the acceptance of truth is an intellectual attitude, however valuable it may be in practice. Wisdom, I shall argue, is preference of merit justified by an evaluation system and undefeated by error. A knowledgeable person is a person who knows much of what she accepts, and a wise person is a person who is wise about much of what she prefers; but both knowledge and wisdom begin with particular bits of knowledge and wisdom, knowing this and that which one accepts, and being wise about this and that which one prefers. There is much to explain in these ideas of being justified and undefeated, but I begin where I must with my system of evaluation.

Coherence, Knowledge, and Wisdom

How can a system of acceptances and preferences justify those preferences and acceptances? The simple answer is that it can cohere with them. A coherence theory of knowledge and wisdom is a theory of knowledge and wisdom without basic propositions or ultimate values. Knowledge and wisdom are relativized to a person's system of evaluation, but whether her system is defeated by error depends on the match between that system and reality. First, though, we must understand how justification can be coherence with a system of evaluation, how a system of acceptances and preferences can justify acceptances and preferences that cohere with it at the same time as they confirm and support that system. How is a coherence theory of knowledge and wisdom possible? How can coherence with an evaluation system supply knowledge and wisdom without first premisses?

I begin with knowledge because the stations along the path are marked by my past excursions. I have said before that a person is personally justified in accepting something

[2] Keith Lehrer, *Theory of Knowledge* (Boulder, Colo., and London, 1990); Keith Lehrer, *Metamind* (Oxford, 1990).

if and only if acceptance of it coheres with the acceptance system of the person. I now think that will not suffice, because preferences are also essential to the kind of coherence that yields justified acceptance. Thus, personally justified acceptance, acceptance justified for me, is acceptance that coheres with an evaluation system including preferences, just as personally justified preference, preference justified for me, is preference that coheres with an evaluation system that includes acceptances. Preferences concerning what I accept and acceptances concerning what I prefer are instruments of justification yielding wisdom and knowledge.

Justification

How does coherence with my evaluation system yield personally justified acceptance, acceptance justified for me? I present some slightly modified versions of definitions presented before,[3] not as an explanation, but as something to explain.

> (D1) A system X is an evaluation system of S if and only if X contains states described by statements of the form, 'S accepts that p', attributing to S just those things that S accepts with the objective of accepting what is true and states described by statements of the form 'S prefers that p', attributing to S just those things that S prefers with the objective of preferring what has merit.

This first definition is a modified one incorporating preferences as well as acceptances into the system yielding justified acceptance as well as justified preference. One might wonder why the system contains states of acceptance and preference rather than simply the things accepted and preferred. The answer is that the principles,

> (A) I am worthy of my trust concerning what I accept,

and

[3] Keith Lehrer, *Theory of Knowledge*, pp. 148–9.

(P) I am worthy of my trust concerning what I prefer,

are needed to obtain the conclusions that I am reasonable in accepting that *p* and that I am reasonable in preferring that *p*. Given this, the premiss of my acceptance that *p* or my preference that *p* is also needed. Reasonable acceptance is not sufficient for justified acceptance, but it is necessary for it. Thus, states of acceptance and preference are essential to the justification of the thing accepted or preferred.

This feature of an evaluation system, that it is a system containing states described by statements expressing the fact that a person accepts and prefers the things he does, is an essential feature for the generation of reasonableness and justification from the system. My acceptance of (A) vouches for itself, as does my preference for (P), just as they vouch for the other things that I accept and prefer. But the premisses that I accept and prefer what I do are essential to the argument for the reasonableness of accepting what I do.

Justification is Coherence

The idea that justification is coherence with a background system is formulated in the following definition:

> (D2) *S* is justified in accepting *p* at *t* on the basis of system *X* of *S* at *t* if and only if acceptance of *p* coheres with *X* of *S* at *t*.

Coherence is more than a negative notion of compatibility, however, it is a positive notion of defensibility against objections or, as I have called them, competitors. A competitor to something I accept is a consideration, which, if assumed to be true, would make acceptance less reasonable. Some competitors contradict what one accepts and must be beaten by the background system, while other competitors imply that acceptance is not worthy of trust and may be neutralized by the background system. This idea is formulated in the following definition:

> (D3) Acceptance of *p* coheres with *X* of *S* at *t* if and only

if all competitors of p are beaten or neutralized for S on X at t.

This definition leaves us with the problem of defining the notions of competing, beating, and neutralizing. Assuming a single epistemic notion of comparative reasonableness, I have defined these notions as follows:

(D4) c competes with acceptance of p for S on X at t if and only if it is more reasonable for S to accept that p on the assumption that c is false than on the assumption that c is true, on the basis of X at t.

(D5) Acceptance of p beats c for S on X at t if and only if c competes with acceptance of p for S on X at t, and it is more reasonable for S to accept p than to accept c on X at t.

(D6) n neutralizes c as a competitor of acceptance of p for S on X at t if and only if c competes with p for S on X at t, the conjunction of c and n does not compete with p for S on X at t, and it is as reasonable for S to accept the conjunction of c and n as to accept c alone on X at t.

Personal Justification

These definitions treat the background system as a variable for the sake of generality. Substitution of the evaluation system for the variable X gives us the definition of personal justification as follows:

(D7) S is personally justified in accepting that p at t if and only if S is justified in accepting that p on the basis of the evaluation system of S at t.

This is an abbreviated version of a theory of justification that I have defended against various objections for a number of years. It is clear that we must add that such justification is not defeated by errors in the evaluation system if it is to convert the acceptance of truth into knowledge. I shall define undefeated justification later in the chapter, but its purpose is to connect justification with truth. Errors break the connection between personal justification and truth and block the conversion to knowledge.

I note some advantages of this coherence theory of justification. Coherence is a relationship defined in terms of comparative reasonableness which holds between what a person accepts and her evaluation system. It is not a global feature of the system. To convert coherence into knowledge, the truth of what is accepted to beat or neutralize competitors will be required for the justification to be undefeated, but coherence and personal justification do not themselves require that external constraint. Coherence itself does not depend on global features of the system nor on external constraints which are inaccessible to the subject. Moreover, coherence supplies a unified account of justification across the field of diverse subjects. The account is thus unified with respect to perceptual knowledge, mathematical knowledge, and even moral knowledge. If what a person accepts coheres with her evaluation system, then she obtains personal justification which, when undefeated by error, will convert to knowledge whatever the content of what she accepts. Others have thought that perceptual and mathematical knowledge require some conditions beyond coherence and truth to yield a satisfactory theory of justification and knowledge. They commit themselves to requiring something beyond coherence for justification. The result is a patchwork of heterogeneous factors rather than a unified coherence theory of justification and knowledge. They are wrong to so commit themselves. Coherence and truth suffice for justification and knowledge.

What now seems to me important is to offer some account of the undefined notion of comparative reasonableness, for that is something that I have taken as primitive, though supplemented with some explanation. A partial explanation is that, other things being equal, the more probable is the more reasonable, but differences in content and explanatory power render things unequal. It may be more reasonable to accept a powerful explanatory theory than some trivial claim, not because explanation is more important than truth, but because powerful explanatory theories, if true, imply more truths than trivial claims, if true. I contend that truth is the fundamental objective of acceptance, for explanations that are false explain nothing, and hypotheses with high informative content that are false give us only a great deal of misinformation. The value of explanatory power and informative content is the value of the amount of truth contained in such power and content if the claim or hypothesis is true.

This view is personal, however, a feature of my evaluation system, and thus supplementary rather than essential to the account of personal justification I am developing here. I think that truth is the fundamental intellectual objective and that other intellectual objectives are merely instrumental to it. Thus, I prefer to accept those things that I have adequate evidence for thinking are true and to eschew acceptance of those things where I lack such evidence; but that is simply a remark about my evaluation system, not a remark about evaluation systems in general. My intellectual preferences are preferences for accepting something if and only if it is true, and I have given my reasons for such preferences. Others may have different preferences. Who has knowledge will depend on the consequences of correcting error in our respective evaluation systems.

Reasonableness and the Keystone

The substitution of an evaluation system for an acceptance system permits us to give an account of the comparative notion of intellectual or theoretical reasonableness in terms of preference. Simply formulated:

> (TR) It is more reasonable for S to accept p than q at t if and only if S prefers accepting p to accepting q and S is worthy of S's trust in this preference.

This thesis, (TR), depends on the argument from the trustworthiness of my preference contained in the last chapter, and thus on the keystone loop. The argument would proceed, however, as follows:

(P) I am worthy of my trust concerning what I prefer.
(1) I prefer accepting p to accepting q to obtain my intellectual objectives.
(2) Acceptance of p is more worthy of my trust than acceptance of q to obtain my intellectual objectives.
(3) Acceptance of p is more reasonable for me than acceptance of q to obtain my intellectual objectives.
(4) It is more reasonable for me to accept p than to accept q to obtain my intellectual objectives.

It is clear, however, that my acceptance of p is essential to the argument as well as the preference expressed in (1), that my preference for the truth of p is essential to the truth of p, that the entire argument depends on the truth of p, and thus that the conclusion of the argument and the correlation expressed in (TR) depend on the keystone loop and are supported by it.

There are other ways to elucidate the role of the keystone loop in theoretical justification. There are myriads of competitors to anything I accept—for example, that I have a blue cup in front of me, which I do—competitors about local illusions, hallucinatory experiences, brains in vats, powerful deceptive demons, and the like. Most of these competitors are beaten because it is more reasonable for me to accept that I see a blue cup than that I am deceived by a demon, for, as I seek truth, I prefer accepting that I see a cup to accepting that I am deceived by a demon. I prefer this in order to obtain my goal of accepting something if and only if it is true. I am, moreover, worthy of my trust concerning my preference, and the reasonableness of that preference for acceptance is held together by the keystone loop.

It becomes clear that the most basic objections to what I accept are objections to what I accept in the keystone loop, namely, that I am worthy of my trust concerning what I accept and prefer, especially what I prefer to accept. That I am not worthy of my trust concerning my acceptance of things or my preference for accepting them is a fundamental competitor or objection to everything that I accept. Thus, for me to be justified in accepting anything, the competitor—that I am not worthy of my trust concerning what I accept—must be beaten. This means that it must be more reasonable for me to accept that I am worthy of my trust concerning what I accept than that I am not, and, thus, I must prefer accepting that I am worthy of my trust concerning what I prefer to accepting that I am not. However, and more deeply, if acceptance of my trustworthiness is no more reasonable than non-acceptance, if, in effect, there is a tie between acceptance and non-acceptance of my trustworthiness, and thus a lack of preference between them, that is also a competitor. For if I have no evaluation of whether I am trustworthy or not, if I cannot say whether I am trustworthy or not in what I accept, that is itself an objection to my accepting the things I do. The keystone loop is essential to meeting the objections to what I accept and, therefore, is required to hold personal justification together. The keystone loop of reasonable acceptance is, therefore, equally a keystone loop of justified acceptance.

There is, however, a difference between the role of the keystone loop in justified acceptance and reasonable acceptance. The difference is that the keystone loop suffices for reasonable acceptance but not for justified acceptance. Though I am worthy of trust in what I accept, I may, nevertheless, accept something which has a competitor that is neither beaten nor neutralized. The defence against all competitors essential to personal justification is not essential to reasonable acceptance. Reasonable acceptance is a step into the life of reason that may fall short of providing the justification needed to convert true acceptance into knowledge when undefeated by error. Consider, for example, the claim that there is intelligent life outside the solar system. I think that I am reasonable to accept that, but I lack the sort of justification required for knowledge, even if I am correct in all that I accept pertaining to such matters. There are objections, competitors, such as that there is no known communication or other evidence of the existence of such creatures that I accept. I consider it reasonable to accept the existence of such intelligent beings on the general grounds that it seems very difficult for me to suppose that we are a unique cosmic accident, but that is not sufficient for knowledge even if I am quite correct in this, for I have no way of beating or neutralizing the objection, which I accept as correct, that there is no empirical evidence of the existence of such beings.

Wisdom and Knowledge

It will be illuminating to compare knowledge to wisdom. I know that something I accept is true if my personal justification for accepting it converts into knowledge when the justification is undefeated by error. I am wise in preferring something if my personal justification for preferring it converts into wisdom when the justification is undefeated by error. My personal justification of preference, like my personal justification of acceptance, is based on my evaluation system. Personal justification of preference, like acceptance, is the result of coherence with the evaluation system consisting of acceptances and preferences. Coherence with a system is the result of defending that preference or acceptance against objections or competitors. As in the case of acceptance, there are two different kinds of objections or competitors to something I prefer. One kind of competitor is an alternative that contradicts the preferred alternative, and another sort of competitor, though consistent with the alternative preferred, states or implies that I am not worthy of my own trust in what I prefer. If the contradictory alternative has greater merit, then I am not justified in preferring the alternative I do prefer; and if I am not trustworthy in preferring what I do, perhaps because I cannot tell whether one alternative has greater merit than the other, then, again, I am not justified in preferring what I do.

Justified Preference

Coherence and justification are based on a comparative notion of reasonableness, on whether one thing is more reasonable than another on the basis of an evaluation system. Whether I am justified in preferring something, like when I am justified in accepting something, depends on how reasonable it is in comparison to objections or competitors. I can conclude that it is more reasonable for me to accept p than a competitor q if I prefer accepting p to accepting q for the purpose of obtaining truth and avoiding error. An arc in the keystone loop of reason is revealed when we note that the conclusion that it is more reasonable for me to accept p than to accept q rests on my acceptance of the premiss of my trustworthiness concerning what I prefer, and, extending ourselves further along the circumference of the loop, on my trustworthiness in accepting this. If my preference for accepting p over accepting q is worthy of my trust, then the preference is reasonable, and therefore, it is more reasonable for me to prefer accepting p than to prefer accepting q.

Another arc in the loop of reason is revealed when we consider what makes it more reasonable for me to prefer that x than to prefer that y. I can conclude that it is more reasonable to prefer that x than to prefer that y if I prefer this and am trustworthy in what I prefer. But again this conclusion depends on my accepting that I am trustworthy in what I prefer and, indeed, on my being trustworthy in what I prefer. As we noted, closing the loop, my being trustworthy in what I prefer depends itself on my preference for being trustworthy in this way. Thus, when I define, as I shall now do, justified preference in terms of comparative reasonableness of preference, comparative reasonableness may be explained within the keystone loop.

Justified Preference Defined

I begin again with the most general account of justified preference of a person on the basis of a background system, as follows:

(DP2) *S* is justified in preferring *p* at *t* on the basis of system *X* of *S* at *t* if and only if preference for *p* coheres with *X* of *S* at *t*.

Coherence with a background system consists of defence against all competitors on the basis of the system, as in the case of acceptance. I shall appeal to the notion of an alternative to a preference as something that contradicts the proposition preferred. Thus, an alternative to my preference that I go to a movie at a given time would be that I not go to that movie at that time but go to another movie then instead.

To defend a preferred alternative it need not be shown that it is better or more reasonable to prefer it than any other alternative. It suffices that my preferred alternative be as good as any alternative and hence as reasonable to prefer. For example, having ordered a meal, I prefer to use a specific ten-dollar bill to pay for the meal. It suffices that the preference for using that ten-dollar bill is not less reasonable than paying with a second ten-dollar bill that I possess. It is not necessary that the ten-dollar bill I prefer to use to pay for the meal be one that it is more reasonable for me to prefer than the second, or that it be better that I use the first than the second. It suffices that the preference for the ten-dollar bill I prefer be as reasonable or not be less reasonable than any other. Thus, coherence may result from evaluating my preference to be as reasonable as any alternative. We shall see, however, that not every competitor to preferring something is an alternative, for, as in the case of acceptance, there are things that make it less reasonable to prefer something without contradicting the preference.

The remaining definitions of justified preference are as follows:

(DP3) Preference for *p* coheres with *X* of *S* at *t* if and only if all competitors of *p* are beaten or neutralized for *S* on *X* at *t*.

(DP4) *c* competes with preference for *p* for *S* on *X* at *t* if and only if it is more reasonable for *S* to prefer that *p* on the assumption that c is false than on the assumption that c is true, on the basis of X at t.

(DP5) Preference for p beats c for S on X at t if and only if c competes with p for S on X at t, and it is more reasonable for S to prefer p than to accept c on X at t.

(DP6) n neutralizes c as a competitor of p for S on X at t if and only if c competes with preference for p for S on X at t, the conjunction of c and n does not compete with preference for p for S on X at t, and it is as reasonable for S to accept the conjunction of c and n as to accept c alone on X at t.

These definitions enable us to define personally justified preference when we replace the variable X with the evaluation system of S.

(DP7) S is personally justified in preferring that p at t if and only if S is justified in preferring that p on the basis of the evaluation system of S at t.

When personal justification is undefeated it converts to wisdom.

Much of what we have said about personal justification of acceptance transfers to our account of personal justification of preference. Competitors are objections that I must meet, and they are met by being beaten or neutralized on the basis of my evaluation system. Preference, like acceptance, can be reasonable but fall short of being personally justified because not all competitors are beaten or neutralized. Moreover, my accepting and preferring that I am trustworthy concerning what I accept and prefer is what converts preference based on an evaluation system into reasonable preference. A fundamental competitor that must be beaten or neutralized is the competitor affirming that I am not trustworthy in what I prefer.

However, comparison of the definitions concerning justified preference and justified acceptance reveals an important difference. Coherence concerning acceptances is solely a matter of whether it is more reasonable to accept one thing than another, and one might expect that coherence concerning preferences would be solely a matter of whether it is more reasonable to prefer one thing than another. The reader might expect an exact parallel between the definitions of beating and neutralizing pertaining to acceptance and preference, that is, between (D6) and (DP6), on the one hand, and (D5) and (DP5), on the other, with preference being uniformly substituted for acceptance throughout. That expectation is not fulfilled. Ekstrom has ably articulated such a theory, however.[4] Had I adopted that proposal, we would have obtained:

> (DP5*) Preference for p beats c for S on X at t if and only if c competes with p for S on X at t, and it is more reasonable for S to prefer p than to *prefer c* on X at t.

> (DP6*) n neutralizes c as a competitor of p for S on X at t if and only if c competes with preference for p for S on X at t, the conjunction of c and n does not compete with preference for p for S on X at t, and it is as reasonable for S to *prefer* the conjunction of c and n as to *prefer c* alone on X at t.

The italicized occurrences of *prefer* would have replaced occurrences of *accept* in (DP5) and (DP6), but it is (DP5) and (DP6) that I advocate and that seem to be yield the proper account of justified preference rather than (DP5*) and (DP6*).

Acceptance and Justified Preference

The reason for the appeal to the reasonableness of accepting things in the definitions pertaining to justified preference is that objections to preferences are not restricted to other preferences, but to what one might accept about other preferences, about other alternatives, and, most crucially, about the trustworthiness of a person concerning what the person prefers and other conditions pertaining to

[4] Laura Waddell Ekstrom, 'A Coherence Theory of Autonomy', *Philosophy and Phenomenological Research*, 53 (1993), 599–616.

the competence of the person to evaluate the worth, merit, or value of alternatives.

For example, there are objections to my preference for writing this chapter now that run as follows:

(1) It would be better for your health to get some exercise than to write this chapter now.

(2) It would be better for all concerned if you wrote less and hence did not write this chapter.

(3) You are being deceived about the merits of the alternatives you consider by an evil demon who controls your thoughts and evaluations in order to get you to write philosophy all the time.

(4) You are a brain in a vat and your thoughts and evaluations are completely controlled by a scientist who makes you think and evaluate as you do by typing the thoughts he wishes you to have on a computer which controls the states of the brain.

(5) You are not worthy of your own trust as you evaluate ends that you consider pursuing.

These are all objections to my preference, objections of different sorts, but all of them are competitors, in the sense that my preference for writing this chapter would be more reasonable if I were to assume that they were false than if I were to assume that they were true. They are all, moreover, things a person might say if she wished to raise sceptical doubts in my mind about my preference for writing this chapter. All these objections or competitors are ones that are beaten or neutralized on the basis of my evaluation system. Competitors (2) to (5) are beaten (though I concede some sceptical discomfort over the claim that (2) is beaten), for I accept and prefer to accept things that imply the falsity of these claims. Competitor (1) is not beaten but is neutralized by the claim that I can achieve the same benefits to my health by exercising in a few hours and writing this chapter now.

Objections (2) to (5) are beaten because preferring to write this book is more reasonable for me than accepting

those things. The comparison of the reasonableness of preference to the reasonableness of acceptance might seem
odd, until one recalls that preferences, like acceptances, are
evaluations. My preference for writing this chapter now requires my evaluation of the merit of doing so, and implies
my acceptance of the merit. Preferences imply acceptance
of the merit of the preferred thing, thus revealing another
loop between preference and acceptance. We must prefer to
accept what we do for it to be reasonable to accept what we
do, and we must accept that what we prefer is as meritorious as any alternative for it to be reasonable to prefer what
we do.

It is time to address a standard objection summarized
and discussed by Kagan.[5] Suppose that I prefer to spend $7
on a movie instead of giving $7 to Oxfam. Is it not obvious
that giving $7 to Oxfam is more meritorious than spending
$7 a movie? Suppose that it is more meritorious to give the
$7 to Oxfam. Then, the objection continues, it is more reas-
onable to give $7 to Oxfam, and I am not reasonable in pre-
ferring to go to the movies. But many of the things we
spend our money on are less meritorious than giving our
money to Oxfam. Might we not be justified in spending our
money as we do, however trivial our pursuits?

My reply may offer some illumination of the notion of
merit that I have used without any definition. The merit of
an alternative is its worth or value. It is tempting to immediately identify the merit, worth, or value of something
with its moral merit, worth, or value, and, though such an
identification is consistent and appealing, most of us do
not, in fact, accept such an identification no matter how enthusiastically we may commend those who do. I may be
convinced that a person giving his or her money to Oxfam,
and restricting his or her expenditures to those necessary
for sustenance and health in order to maximize the amount
given to Oxfam, is admirable and saintly, but I do not agree
that the preferences of such a person have greater merit

[5] Shelly Kagan, *The Limits of Morality* (Oxford, 1989).

than my own, though I agree they have greater moral merit. There is more to merit than morals. There is the merit of individual freedom and its exercise, for example. The merit of exercising one's freedom may conflict with the moral claims of others, and it is difficult, as any thoughtful person knows, to decide between them. One can decide the matter on its merits, however. Similarly, there can be conflict, as Heil as emphasized, between epistemic and moral considerations which, again, may be decided on the merits of the issue.[6] The merit of an alternative will depend on our objectives and upon other matters. The notion of merit, like that of truth, is not one I am able to define in a satisfactory way, for any definition I might offer would define merit in terms of worth or some other notion of value, just as a definition of truth would define truth in terms of meaning or some other notion of semantics, and such definitions are likely to be controversial, unilluminating, or both. Fortunately, we can often decide the merit or truth of something without being able to define either notion.

What we accept about the merit of things yields the consequence that preferring something is more reasonable than accepting an objection to preferring it, for example, when we accept that preferring what we do has greater merit than accepting the objections to it. Moreover, the reasonableness of preferring one alternative to another is the result of our acceptance of the greater merit of preferring the one to the other. The comparative reasonableness of preferring one thing to another on the basis of our evaluation system is a consequence of our accepting that the preferred thing is meritorious, and, of course, on our acceptance of the trustworthiness of what we thus accept. I leave you to close the loop.

It is obvious that justified acceptance and justified preference rest on the keystone of our evaluation system just as acceptance and preference support the keystone of our trustworthiness. The things I accept support the conclusion

⁶ John Heil, 'Believing Reasonably', *Nous*, 26 (1992), 47–62.

that I am worthy of my trust concerning the set of things I accept and prefer, where this set includes a loop of my acceptance and preference for this conclusion. My preference for my being worthy of my trust concerning these matters reinforces the loop. In spite of my insistence on the importance of the loop, it is essential to note the importance of all the acceptances and preferences of the system. We must incorporate these evaluations of what is true and what has merit in order to sustain the support of the keystone loop which holds the system together.

The claim that I am worthy of my trust concerning what I accept and prefer is both premiss and conclusion of a system tied together in a loop of acceptances, preferences, and reasonings. But that premiss and conclusion are supported by a theory of how we can best attain truth, of what counts as a best effort to attain truth, of what results in success and what does not. Similarly, it is supported by a background theory of how we can obtain what has merit or worth, of what counts as a best effort to attain what has worth, of what results in success and what does not.

Over time the theory is modified, and with these modifications we also modify how we change what we accept and prefer as well as how we reason about these things. So far, our conception has been synchronic, static, fixed to a point in time and our evaluation system at that time. We shall eventually transcend this perspective and accept the importance of doing so, but first a consideration of what we obtained from self-trust and our acceptance and preference for our trustworthiness.

Undefeated Justification: Knowledge

Personally justified acceptance and preference are the basis of an account of knowledge and wisdom, but they do not by themselves constitute either. They are based on an evaluation system, on mine, for example, and whether I know the thing I am personally justified in accepting, or whether I am wise about the thing I am personally justified in preferring, will depend on whether I have met the objections to what I accept or prefer on basis of error or on the basis of truth. Personal justification undefeated by error converts into knowledge and wisdom. I have advanced a notion of undefeated justified acceptance as follows:

(D8) S is justified in accepting that p at t in a way that is undefeated if and only if S is justified in accepting p at t on the basis of every system that is a member of the ultrasystem (defined in (D10) below) of S at t.

(D9) M defeats the personal justification of S for accepting p at t if and only if S is personally justified in accepting p at t, but S is not justified in accepting p at t on system M at t where M is a member of the ultrasystem of S at t.

(D10) A system M is a member of the ultrasystem of S at t if and only if either (a) M is the evaluation system of S at t or results from (b) eliminating one or more states described by statements of the form 'S accepts that q' when q is false, (c) replacing one or more states described by statements of the form 'S accepts that q' when q is false with a state described by statement of the form 'S accepts that not-q', or (d) any combination of such eliminations and replacements in the evaluation system of S at t with the constraint that if q logically entails r, which is false and also accepted, then the state described by 'S accepts that r' must be also be eliminated or replaced just as was the state that described 'S accepts that q'.

These definitions yield the following definition of knowledge:

(DK) S knows that p at t if and only if (i) S accepts that p, (ii) it is true that p, (iii) S is personally justified in accepting that p at t, and (iv) S is justified in accepting that p at t in a way that is undefeated.

Condition (iv) implies condition (iii); and interpreting (iv) so that (iv) implies (i), it will imply (ii) as well by the transitivity of implication. So, we may obtain the following reduction of the analysis:

(DK*) *S* knows that *p* at *t* if and only if *S* is justified in accepting that *p* at *t* in a way that is undefeated.

Hence, knowledge becomes undefeated justification.

The intuitive idea behind these definitions is that there are two ways of correcting an acceptance of something false in my evaluation system. Suppose I accept that *p* and, hence, my acceptance of *p'* is a member of my evaluation system. Now suppose that it is false that *p*, and so my acceptance is an error. How might someone correct this error in my evaluation system? There are two ways. One is to substitute my acceptance of not-*p'*, and the other is just to delete my acceptance of *p* and let it go at that. However my error might be corrected, I only know those things that stand up, that remain justified, on the basis of the resulting corrected system. That is what these definitions tell us. Personal justification converts into knowledge only if it remains when either weak or strong corrections are made in my evaluation system.

Undefeated Justification: Wisdom

So much for acceptance, but what about preference? Do we need to correct preferences as well as acceptances to test for knowledge and wisdom? I think that the way in which preference and acceptance are based on each other obviates the need for that. If I prefer an alternative, prefer that *p*, and I am personally justified in this preference, then I can answer all objections to this preference, including the objection that there is a better alternative, which requires accepting that there is no better alternative or something equally potent for replying to the objection. Now suppose that this is false. A strong correction of my evaluation system substituting a state described by:

I accept that there is a better alternative than preferring that *p*, for one described by:

> I accept that there is no better alternative than preferring that p,

will result in a failure to obtain justification for the preference that p on the basis of the system with the strong correction of erroneous acceptance just made. I assume that personally justified preference is based on acceptances in the evaluation system. If all these acceptances are true, personally justified preference constitutes wisdom, with regard to at least that preference.

We can formulate this condition with a simple amendment of definitions (D8) and (D9), leaving the complicated (D10) as is:

> (DP8) S is justified in preferring that p at t in a way that is undefeated if and only if S is justified in preferring that p at t on the basis of every system that is a member of the ultrasystem of S at t.
>
> (DP9) M defeats the personal justification of S for preferring that p at t if and only if S is personally justified in preferring that p at t, but S is not justified in preferring that p at t on system M at t where M is a member of the ultrasystem (as defined in (D10) above) of S at t.

These definitions yield the following definition of wisdom in terms of preference:

> (DW) S is wise in preferring that p at t if and only if (i) S prefers that p, (ii) S is personally justified in preferring that p at t, and (iii) S is justified in preferring that p at t in a way that is undefeated.

Condition (iii) implies conditions (ii) and (i). So, we may obtain the following reduction of the analysis:

> (DW*) S is wise in preferring that p at t if and only if S is justified in preferring that p at t in a way that is undefeated.

Wisdom concerning preference is undefeated justified preference, just as knowledge concerning acceptance is undefeated justified acceptance.

The notion of being a member of the ultrasystem is just a notion of the system resulting from weak or strong corrections in the evaluation system of the person as explained above. The novelty of this account of wisdom is that it is based on the assumption that practical wisdom is based on justification resulting from being undefeated by any error in what a person accepts. There is no truth condition in the definition of wise preference, for one can prefer something and be wise in so doing, even though one does not obtain what one prefers; but the role of truth in wisdom is otherwise the same as in knowledge, and the two are again looped together.

There is no truth condition in the definition of wise preference. To know that p, it must be true that p when I accept that, but to wisely prefer that p, it need not be true that p when I prefer that p. But the role of truth in wisdom is as robust as the role of truth in knowledge when one considers what is required for justification to be undefeated. Mistakes about the consequences and character of what I prefer may defeat my personal justification for my preference, and, therefore, accepting what is true about the consequences and character may be an essential prophylactic against defeat. Moreover, if I accept that the preference has merit when it does not, then, assuming there is a truth of the matter about what has merit, my error about the merit of my preference may again defeat my justification for preferring it.

Is there a truth of the matter about what has merit? I assume there is. Suppose a sceptic denies this. What can I say? I can note that if the sceptic is right, then silence in philosophical discussion seems the appropriate response. For, if I offer an argument against the claim of another, but go on to concede that there is no more merit to my argument than that of my opponent because there is no truth of the matter about the merit of anything, argumentation included, the point of argument seems to evaporate in sub-

jectivity and had better end. If my opponent demurs at this
suggestion, and contends that the merit is on her side even
though there is no truth of the matter about where the
merit rests, I would prefer bemused silence to further dis-
putation. I leave it open how to define truth concerning
matters of merit as well as concerning other matters, for
reasons I shall consider in the next chapter.[7] The role of
truth in wisdom is the same as that of knowledge pertaining to the role of undefeated justification in both. The merit
of my preferences concerning what I accept, and my acceptance of the merit of what I prefer, are essential to the undefeated justification of both knowledge and wisdom, and
loop the two together.

The Transformation Argument

The loop reveals itself again when one poses the question
of why we do not require correction of preferences as well
as correction of acceptances in the analysis of wisdom or,
for that matter, in the analysis of knowledge. Preference for
what lacks merit can lead us astray quite as easily as acceptance of what lacks truth. The reply is that justified preference based on error, like justified acceptance based on
error, will be defeated. But cannot a person have a system
of preferences that are not worthy of her trust and yet not
based on any errors?

Any preference that is justified must be more reasonable
than the objections raised against it, including the objection
that the person's preferences are not worthy of her trust.
Thus, a person is not personally justified in her preferences
unless it is more reasonable for her to prefer what she does
than to accept that she is not worthy of her trust in her pref-

---

[7] For anyone interested in the debate about whether claims about
what has merit have truth values, the classic articles and major con-
tenders can be found in Geoffrey Sayre-McCord's collection, *Essays on
Moral Realism* (Ithaca, N.Y., 1988). Discussion of the relation between
knowledge and wisdom can be found in Keith Lehrer, Jeannie Lum,
Beverly Slichta, and Nicholas Smith (eds.), *Knowledge, Teaching, and
Wisdom* (Boston, Mass., 1996).

erences; and thus, she must accept something to the effect that she is worthy of her trust in her preferences, for her preference to be justified on the basis of her evaluation system.

Assume a person is not worthy of her trust in her preferences, though she accepts that she is. Once the error concerning this matter is strongly corrected by substituting a state descrbed by:

I accept that I am not worthy of my trust in my preferences,

for one described by:

I accept that I am worthy of my trust in my preferences,

which is contained in her original evaluation system, her personal justification for her preference based on her evaluation system will be defeated by the member of her ultrasystem that corrects the error.

This argument is important, and similar to the argument in defence of the idea that undefeated justified acceptance is knowledge. The objection is that the system of acceptances might be isolated from reality in some exotic way, perhaps because our senses do not influence what we accept due to deception or dysfunction. But our reply is that personal justification requires that such objections or competitors be met, and to meet them one must accept that one is not so isolated, or something to that effect; and this acceptance, if false, will result in the justification being defeated.

I have called this argument the *transformation* argument because it concerns the transformation of justified acceptance into undefeated justified acceptance, and the same point pertains to justified preference and the transformation of it into undefeated justified preference. Raise a sceptical doubt and that doubt must be met by the evaluation system of a person for her to obtain personal justification. To meet it, she must accept a reply. If the doubt is correct and the reply is in error, the error will defeat the justification.

Thus, the analysis ensures that wisdom and knowledge must be based on truth that transforms justified acceptance and preference into knowledge and justification.

The crux of the argument pertaining to justified preference and wisdom is that justified preference is based on the acceptance of views about what preferences have merit. It is also based on the assumption that I am worthy of my trust in what I accept about what has merit. One of the things I accept concerns the merit of being trustworthy in what I accept as true. As a result I prefer to be trustworthy in what I accept. Justified preference rests on acceptance of my trustworthiness in what I prefer, and justified acceptance rests on my preference for being trustworthy, and that shows how the keystone loop ties knowledge and wisdom together. I accept the necessity of preferring to be trustworthy in what I accept, and prefer to achieve the trustworthiness that I accept as necessary to undefeated justification in theory and practice. Undefeated justification in theory and practice is, as we have seen, knowledge and wisdom. That is how it is all looped together.

FOR FURTHER READING

On theories of justification and knowledge:

Bender, John W. (ed.), *The Current State of the Coherence Theory* (Boston and Dordrecht: Kluwer Academic Publishers, 1989).

BonJour, Laurence, *The Structure of Empirical Knowledge* (Cambridge, Mass.: Harvard University Press, 1985).

Chisholm, Roderick, *Theory of Knowledge*, 3rd edn. (Englewood Cliffs, N.J.: Prentice-Hall, 1989).

Cohen, Stewart, 'Justification and Truth', *Philosophical Studies*, 46 (1984), 279–95.

Dretske, Fred, *Knowledge and the Flow of Information* (Cambridge, Mass.: MIT Press, 1981).

Falvey, Kevin, and Joseph Owens, 'Externalism, Self-Knowledge, and Skepticism', *Philosophical Review*, 103 (1994), 107–37.

Foley, Richard, *A Theory of Epistemic Rationality* (Cambridge, Mass.: Harvard University Press, 1987).

Gettier, Edmund Jr., 'Is Justified True Belief Knowledge?', *Analysis*, 23 (1963), 121–3.

Goldman, Alvin I., *Epistemology and Cognition* (Cambridge, Mass.: Harvard University Press, 1986).

Klein, Peter, *Certainty: A Refutation of Scepticism* (Minneapolis, Minn.: University of Minnesota Press, 1981).

Lehrer, Keith, *Theory of Knowledge* (Boulder, Colo., and London: Westview Press and Routledge, 1990).

—— *Metamind* (Oxford: Clarendon Press, 1990).

Moser, Paul K., *Knowledge and Evidence* (New York: Cambridge University Press, 1989).

Nozick, Robert, *Philosophical Explanations* (Cambridge, Mass.: Harvard University Press, 1981).

Plantinga, Alvin, *Warrant and Proper Function* (New York: Oxford University Press, 1993).

Pollock, John, *Contemporary Theories of Knowledge* (Totowa, N.J.: Rowman & Littlefield, 1986).

Roth, Michael, and Glenn Ross, *Doubting: Contemporary Perspectives on Skepticism* (Boston, Mass.: Kluwer Academic Publishers, 1992).

Sosa, Ernest, *Knowledge in Perspective* (New York: Cambridge University Press, 1991).

Swain, Marshall, *Reasons and Knowledge* (Ithaca, N.Y.: Cornell University Press, 1981).

3

Trustworthiness and Supervenience

This chapter will be concerned with the nature of trustworthiness, that which makes a person worthy of his or her own trust concerning acceptance, preference, and reasoning. The focus of the chapter will be the question of whether trustworthiness concerning acceptance supervenes on naturalistic or non-epistemic features of agents.

To motivate that question and to increase our understanding of trustworthiness, let us recall how we began our study. We began with the basic sequence of self-trust. I trust myself, I am worthy of my trust, and, finally, I am worthy of my trust concerning what I accept, prefer, and how I reason. The sequence could have continued to transcend the present moment, the static or synchronic point of view, to consider change and reach the diachronic dimension. I might continue the sequence by adding that I am worthy of my trust concerning the way in which I change what I accept, prefer, and how I reason, and even beyond that to the way in which I change the way I change what I accept, prefer, and how I reason.

Let me list the sequence as follows:

(S) I trust myself.
(T) I am worthy of my trust.
(APR) I am worthy of my trust concerning what I accept, prefer, and how I reason.
(TC) I am worthy of my trust concerning the way in which I change what I accept, prefer, and how I reason.
(CC) I am worthy of my trust concerning the way in which I change the way in which I change what I ac-

cept, prefer, and how I reason.

A regress threatens here, but it might be ended with a loop by some principle as:

(CL) I am worthy of my trust concerning how I change my ways.

If I use a method to change what I accept, prefer, or how I reason, (CL) will support the conclusion that the change is reasonable, and if I change that method, (CL) will equally support the conclusion that the change of method is reasonable. So whatever method I use to change my methods, if that method is used to change itself, (CL) will yield the conclusion that the change is reasonable. It is said that science is self-correcting. Principle (CL) captures the idea that some method of science, or, at any rate, of my science, corrects itself and supports the conclusion that it is reasonable for me to accept the correction.

Trustworthiness

It is interesting to transform these claims about my being worthy of my trust into claims about my being trustworthy, because trustworthiness is an ability, capacity, or disposition. I am worthy of my trust because of some ability, capacity, or disposition that makes me worthy of my trust. We might say that my being trustworthy is what makes me worthy of my trust. There is, however, an ambiguity that must be resolved concerning the claim that I am trustworthy. When a speaker affirms that someone is trustworthy, one understands the speaker as affirming that the person in question is trustworthy *for the listener* to whom the remark is made. This is important because trustworthiness is a relative notion in the sense that a person can be trustworthy for one person and not for another, just as an instrument can be trustworthy for one person but not for another.

A person or an instrument is trustworthy for a person when the person is aware of the capacity, ability, or disposition of the person or instrument which makes the person or thing worth trusting. When I say that I am trustworthy in this particular context, in which I am reflecting upon whether I am worthy of my trust and express self-trust in the sequence, I mean that I am trustworthy *for me* or *for myself*. I claim that I have the capacity, ability, or disposition that makes me worthy of my trust.

Thus, if I accept the sequence of self-trust articulated above, I should accept the sequence of trustworthiness of the self as follows:

(St) I trust myself.

(Tt) I am trustworthy for myself.

(APRt) I am trustworthy for myself concerning what I accept, prefer, and how I reason.

(TCt) I am trustworthy for myself concerning the way in which I change what I accept, prefer, and how I reason.

(CCt) I am trustworthy for myself concerning the way in which I change the way in which I change what I accept, prefer, and how I reason.

(CLt) I am trustworthy for myself concerning how I change my ways.

What is Trustworthiness?

I am trustworthy concerning what I accept and prefer only when I exercise a capacity to accept what is worth accepting and prefer what is worth preferring. Some consider the notion of trustworthiness and reasonableness concerning acceptance and preference to be solely instrumental, and the capacity of trustworthiness to be a capacity to adjust means to ends. According to this view, which I shall challenge, some end of acceptance is specified: truth; some end of preference: happiness; and trustworthiness and reasonableness are defined in terms of exercising a capacity to adjust means to the end. This is a basic idea behind reliabilism in epistemology and hedonism in ethics.

Instrumentalism: A Critique

The problem with both instrumentalist theories is the same. Suppose you attain the end you choose for which acceptance or preference are your instruments, truth or pleasure. If what you have accepted is true, then you have found what you sought in that case. If what you have preferred maximizes pleasure, then you have attained what you sought in that case. Of course, the way in which you have attained truth or pleasure might not be generally reliable; you might just have been lucky in the particular case and have used some method that generally would not lead to the acceptance of truth or the preference for maximizing pleasure. But that is not a just criticism of the reasonableness of the acceptance or preference in that individual case if the only objective of reasonableness is instrumental, to serve as a means to truth and pleasure. If you have obtained all that you could of truth or pleasure in the particular case of acceptance or preference, and all that matters is getting truth or pleasure, then in that case you have completely succeeded. Therefore, on this theory, you would be trustworthy in what you accept or prefer, and it would be reasonable for you to accept or prefer what you did.

The problem with the theory is that you might, in fact, have succeeded by mere luck and proceeded to accept and prefer what you did on the basis of foolish assumptions and fallacious reasoning. In that case, though you succeeded in attaining your ends in accepting and preferring what you did, what you accepted was not worth accepting or what you preferred was not worth preferring. Your success does not vitiate the fact that your acceptance and preference, however effective as instruments, were not worthy of your trust. You were, consequently, not reasonable to accept or prefer what you did, however fortunate the outcome in terms of your ends.

Moreover, even if the success results from a method or process which is generally reliable, the general reliability might be irrelevant in the particular case. In that event, even though you succeed in accepting or preferring something which fulfils your objectives by a method or process that is generally reliable, your acceptance and preference was, once again, not worthy of your trust. This is most clear in the case in which you have no reason to accept that the test is generally reliable; or perhaps some have reason for thinking that it is not reliable in this instance, but ignore this reason and accept the result anyway.

There is another standard criticism of instrumentalism, which is that the question of the worth of pursuing the end, whether theoretical or practical, is ignored by the theory. If I succeed in attaining some end that was not worth pursuing in the first place, then my attaining the end might not be reasonable. The two objections are closely connected. What I pursue must have worth or I am not trustworthy in pursuing it. If I am not trustworthy in pursuing an end, I might not be reasonable in pursuing it. However, even if an end is worth pursuing, there are ways to pursue the end that have worth and ways that do not.

Trustworthiness: The Worth of Ends and Means

What makes me trustworthy in what I accept and prefer is that I exercise a capacity to accept and prefer what is worth accepting and preferring. That requires a capacity to discern that the ends I pursue in acceptance and preference are worth pursuing, and that the means that I use to pursue those ends are ones that are worth employing. I am not worthy of my trust in my pursuits unless the ends are worthy of my trust, and the means by which I pursue them are worthy of my trust as well.

Reasonable acceptance and preference may be inductively inferred from trustworthiness in what one accepts and prefers. Trustworthiness in what one accepts and prefers depends on the worth of the ends pursued and the worth of the means used to pursue them. May one be reasonable in what one accepts and prefers even if one is not trustworthy in what one accepts and prefers? One reason for thinking that one might be is the possibility of being deceived either naturally or supernaturally in a way that is undetectable. A related reason is that one may be reasonable in accepting something that is false including, for example, that one is pursing something worth pursuing by a method worth using to pursue it. Thus, one may be reasonable in accepting that one is trustworthy in something one accepts or prefers even though, being fallible as we all are, one is not trustworthy in the matter. My trustworthiness for myself in what I accept or prefer provides a premiss from which I may inductively infer my reasonableness in what I accept or prefer. The possibility remains, however, that I am reasonable in accepting or preferring something even though I err in some way about my trustworthiness. Similar remarks apply to personal justification, though I must accept that I am trustworthy and prefer to be so in order to meet the objections to what I accept and prefer and attain such personal justification. To convert personal justification to knowledge and wisdom, however, I must be trustworthy in the matter and not erroneously accept that I am. For such an error would defeat my justification and block the path to knowledge and wisdom.

My trustworthiness is a capacity to accept and prefer what is worth accepting and preferring. Moreover, if I am trustworthy *for myself*, I must be aware of having this capacity as well, and, hence, I must be trustworthy about my trustworthiness to be trustworthy for myself. The loop of my trustworthiness onto itself is the same as the loop of my being worthy of my own trust which we studied in the first chapter.

The familiar criticism of instrumentalism in morals is equally applicable in ethics and epistemology. Success in attaining some goal such as obtaining truth or pleasure is not sufficient for my being worthy of my trust in what I accept or what I prefer. The person who succeeds in causing pleasure by means that are not worthy of her trust is not wise in her preference for the means; and, similarly, a person who succeeds in obtaining truth by means that are not worthy of her trust is not knowledgeable in her acceptance of the means. Acceptance is a necessary means to obtaining what is worth accepting, though it is not sufficient; and preference is a necessary means to obtaining what is worth preferring, though it is not sufficient.

Acceptance and preference are necessary means to reasonable acceptance and preference, to justified acceptance and preference, and, finally, to knowledge and wisdom. Thus, whether I am worthy of my trust in what I accept depends on whether what I accept and prefer is worth accepting and preferring. Whether what I accept and prefer is worth accepting and preferring will, finally, depend on whether the ends that I pursue in accepting and preferring are worth pursuing and whether I pursue them in a way that itself has worth.

Acceptance and preference involve evaluation, and evaluation is a determination of value or worth. The evaluation of worth presupposes an understanding of what has worth. I evaluate what I believe or consider in order to decide whether it is worth accepting, and I evaluate what I desire or contemplate in order to decide whether it is worth preferring to satisfy or pursue. But how do I decide whether something is worth preferring or worth accepting? I must exercise a capacity to evaluate, of course, but I must also consider my evaluation system in the exercise of that capacity. I must decide whether to change what I accept or prefer by adding something to my evaluation system or deleting something from it. Thus, acceptance and preference are evaluations on the basis of my evaluation system that may change the system on which they are based. Changes in what one accepts and prefers are based on what one accepts and prefers. Moreover, a person may accept that some way of changing what she accepts or prefers is worthy of her trust and, therefore, prefer to change what she accepts in that way. She may, as well, accept that some way of changing the way of changing what one accepts or prefers is worthy of her trust and prefer to change the way she changes the way of changing what she accepts and prefers. Put another way, she has a method for changing what she accepts and prefers, and she has a method for changing methods. The same thing applies to how she reasons. This we noted above and articulated as the general principles of change, (CC), (CL), (CCt), and (CLt).

Beyond Rules: The Existential Thesis

A question naturally arises as to whether one can always apply rules of acceptance and preference, rules telling us what to accept and prefer, or whether some things that we accept and prefer must be accepted or preferred autonomously and without rule or method. Sartre has remarked that some choices must be made without justification and without excuse.[1] Much that it is reasonable for me to accept or prefer is reasonable because of the way in which it is based on my evaluation system. Further, I am trustworthy in much of what I accept or prefer because of the way in which it is based on my evaluation system including the keystone loop of acceptance and preference contained therein.

My trustworthiness is not exhausted by rules and methods because there is a point at which I must exercise my autonomy and choose those methods and rules. I shall call this claim about the role of autonomous choice the *existential thesis*. I shall give two arguments in defence of the existential thesis. The first is that trustworthiness does not supervene on some base of acceptance, preference, and other natural states. The point of this argument is that, though our trustworthiness concerning what we accept and prefer depends on our evaluation system of acceptances and preferences, it does not supervene on that system.

The second argument is one based on the inevitability of conflict. An important function or purpose of metamental ascent and higher-order evaluation is conflict resolution.

---

[1] Jean-Paul Sartre, *Being and Nothingness*, trans. Hazel E. Barnes (New York, 1956).

But, I shall argue, conflict resolved by appeal to rules may arise again concerning the rules, and, in fact, the rule may apply to itself, much in the way in which our acceptance of our trustworthiness concerning what we accept applies to itself. The choice to follow the rule is existential, both because it applies to itself and because the conflicts that rules resolve concerning acceptance and preference are conflicts that may arise again concerning the acceptance of the rule and preference for conformity to it. The only way to resolve conflict, therefore, is to exercise one's autonomy and choose. Whether my existential choice is trustworthy depends on whether I am trustworthy, and that depends on me and whether I am autonomous. I shall leave formulation of the second argument until the next chapter and turn here to the issue of supervenience.

Supervenience and Foundationalism

Let me first consider the argument concerning supervenience. My interest in the subject of supervenience and epistemology was aroused by the work of Alston, Van Cleve, and Sosa.[2] They have argued that if epistemic properties supervene on non-epistemic ones, then one argument in favour of coherence theories over foundation theories of justification is undermined. The argument is one to the effect that if the supervenience thesis is correct, then the coherence theorist must sacrifice her primary alleged advantage over any foundation theorist.

That advantage of the coherence theory is that the coherence theorist can explain why our most fundamental beliefs are justified, namely, because they cohere with some system of beliefs, while the foundation theorist is limited to saying that our basic beliefs are justified without giving any explanation of why. Any explanation of why our basic

---

[2] William P. Alston, 'Two Types of Foundationalism', *Journal of Philosophy*, 73 (1976), 165–85; James Van Cleve, 'Foundationalism, Epistemic Principles and the Cartesian Circle', *Philosophical Review*, 88 (1979), 55–91; and Ernest Sosa, *Knowledge in Perspective* (New York, 1991), ch. 10.

beliefs are justified would become the basis of an argument to the conclusion that they are justified, and such an argument would render the justification of the beliefs in question non-basic. The coherence theorist thus claims that the foundation theorist is left with a kind of explanatory surd which the coherence theorist can avoid by explaining justification in terms of coherence. That issue is the one that interests me and which, in fact, convinces me that the coherence theorist should resist the supervenience thesis. I intend to resist and to exhibit my resistance here.

Supervenience

What, however, is the thesis I shall resist? The basic idea behind supervenience can be refined in many different ways, but it is basically a modal thesis. Suppose that S is the supervening property and that B is the base property on which it supervenes. The idea is that for any supervening property S, there is some base property B, such that if something is B, then necessarily it is S. The idea can be modified to allow for the possibility of there being nothing that is S, even though some things are B, by affirming that *if* anything is S, *then* if something is B, it is necessarily S.[3] I shall focus on the simpler and stronger thesis that says that S supervenes on B just in case if anything is B, then necessarily it is S, but I shall comment on the modified thesis as well. I shall concern myself with metaphysical necessity, that is, with forms of necessity that hold across possible worlds and are non-contingent.

I shall restrict myself to arguing that metaphysical supervenience, which has been embraced by a leading foundation theorist, must, in fact, be denied by the coherence theorist to retain the explanatory advantage of the coherence theory. I shall, moreover, argue that there are good reasons for a coherence theorist to reject metaphysical supervenience of the standard variety. I leave open the ques-

[3] Cf. Jaegwon Kim, 'Concepts of Supervenience', *Philosophy and Phenomenological Research*, 45 (1984), 153–76.

tion of whether supervenience based on some form of contingent necessity, characteristic of laws of nature, for example, might hold between epistemic properties and non-epistemic ones.

Foundationalism: A Defence

I have argued that the foundationalist must simply assume some principle of the form

(F) If NBp, then Jp.

where NB is a naturalistic property of basic beliefs and J is a property of justification. To the question, why are we justified in accepting that p if NB of p, the answer is that we just are. I have juxtaposed this position to a coherence theory which, rather then just positing some such principle, offers an explanation as to why we are justified in accepting that p if NB of p, namely, that if NB of p, then p coheres with the appropriate background system and corrected versions thereof.[4]

Van Cleve has objected that the coherence theory itself commits us to a principle that plays the same role as (F) does in the foundations theory.[5] Let NCp say that p coheres with some system in some naturalistic manner required for justification by the coherence theory. Van Cleve's point would be that the coherentist must accept some principle having the same form as (F) where NC is now a coherence property as follows:

(C) If NCp, then Jp.

The coherence theorist can no more answer the question of why we are justified in accepting that p if NC of p than the foundationalist is capable of answering the question directed at (F).

Thus, Van Cleve concludes that the coherence theory

---

[4] Keith Lehrer, *Theory of Knowledge* (Boulder, Colo., and London, 1990)
[5] James Van Cleve, 'Foundationalism, Epistemic Principles and the Cartesian Circle'.

does not have any advantage over the foundations theory. In essence, this argument is that both theories assume that justification supervenes on some non-epistemic property. Both (F) and (C) are claimed to be principles of supervenience, and given that epistemic properties supervene on non-epistemic ones, whether the sort that a foundationalist defends or the sort that a coherence theorist defends, the principle of supervenience is basic. Thus, if some supervenience principle holds, it will, in a sense, be a first principle of justification, and, as a result, there will be no answer to the question of why it is true other than, 'It just is!' It is a kind of epistemic surd. Of course, the principle might generate justified acceptance of claims that could be used to justify the principle itself. It might yield justified premises adequate to conclude that the property of being *NB* or *NC* is a reliable indicator of truth. But again, that does not distinguish the foundations theory from the coherence theory.

This is a formidable argument that Van Cleve has presented in a completely convincing way. The crux is a dilemma. Either justification supervenes on a non-epistemic property or it does not. If it does, then we can obtain justified premises as a result of supervenience and use them to justify the principle of supervenience on either kind of theory. If justification does not supervene on any non-epistemic property, then we cannot obtain justified premises on either theory.

Coherence and Supervenience

I wish to take the second horn of the dilemma. I have defined coherence in terms of a comparative notion of reasonableness, to wit, that it is more reasonable for a person to accept one thing rather than another on the basis of an evaluation system of the person, and, therefore, I am not committed to holding that justification supervenes on any non-epistemic property. The notion of comparative reasonableness based on a system is an epistemic notion, not a naturalistic one. In short, it is open to a coherence theorist to argue that coherence is itself an epistemic notion, and, therefore, to reject any principle of the form of (C) above as metaphysically necessary. There is, she might argue, no principle of the supervenience of the epistemic on the non-epistemic. There is no exit from the epistemic loop.

One central motive for defending a coherence theory is precisely the rejection of the supervenience thesis. It is not the case that the coherence theorist rejects the supervenience thesis after noticing that acceptance of it leaves her with a principle that is as basic as the principles of basic belief on the foundations theory. It is, rather, that the coherence theorist notes that either we must accept some principle of supervenience without explanation, or we shall ultimately appeal to a system of beliefs for the justification of any belief and, thus, finally close the loop. I, as a coherence theorist, choose the second alternative. The claim of the coherence theorist, though not only the coherence theorist, is that the principles connecting the non-epistemic with the epistemic are not necessary but contingent. Sosa formulates this doctrine by saying the epistemic is autonomous from the non-epistemic and does not supervene thereupon.[6] I prefer to say that the epistemic is metaphysically *independent* of the non-epistemic in order preserve the notion of *autonomy* for other purposes. It is the great merit of Van Cleve, Alston, and Sosa that they showed us why a coherence theorist should accept the independence thesis.

Naturalistic Coherence

First some remarks about the consequences for a coherence theory of accepting that (C) is necessary and that justification supervenes on non-epistemic properties of coherence. The only difference between the supervenient coherence theory and the supervenient foundations theory would be that the former maintains that justification supervenes on a coherence relation to a system of non-epistemic things rather than supervening on any single non-epistemic item

[6] Ernest Sosa, *Knowledge in Perspective*, ch. 10.

as a foundations theory might hold. This is not a trivial difference. A coherence theorist might hold that the system which generates justification contains a non-epistemic relationship to principle (C) itself.

The coherence theorist might claim, for example, that something like the following is true:

> (CSR) If S has an evaluation system A which contains (CSR) and p n-coheres with A, then S is justified in accepting that p.

If 'n-coheres' were defined non-epistemically, perhaps in terms of some naturalistic probability relation such as relative truth frequency, this principle could be construed as a principle of supervenience assuming that all statements of the form 'S accepts that p' and 'S prefers that p' are non-epistemic. The assumption that all such statements are non-epistemic seems reasonable even if what substitutes for 'p' is epistemic. The statement that a person accepts that God exists is a naturalistic psychological statement about the person rather than a supernaturalistic statement about God. Acceptance, even of epistemic or supernatural content, is a non-epistemic natural state. So is preference.

Let us call (CSR) a naturalized coherence theory. Notice that if (CSR) n-coheres with A, then S is justified in accepting (CSR). Whether this is the case might depend on what A contains, but it would be an account where we would not be driven to the epistemic surd. We can answer the question of why a person is justified in accepting something that n-coheres with her evaluation system. The answer is that (CSR) says so. The foundationalist can make a similar remark when asked why we are justified in accepting something that has NB, to wit, that is what (F) tells us. But the foundationalist is committed to the surd when asked why we are justified in accepting what (F) tells us.

On the other hand, when the naturalized coherence theorist is asked why we are justified in accepting the things that (CSR) tells us we are justified in accepting, she can reply that we are justified in accepting (CSR) because (CSR) n-coheres with our evaluation system and is contained therein. The coherence theory loops around the surd in the keystone loop. The principle of justification together with other things we accept, for example, that n-coherence with an evaluation system yields truth, loops back to the result that we are justified in accepting the principle itself. One might complain of the circularity of this, but it seems to me a virtue of a theory of justification that it should vouch for itself in a justificatory loop tying it together with other things that we accept. The naturalized coherence theorist may favour the loop over the surd and the regress.

Self-Justification

Is this observation enough of a defence of the coherence theorist over the foundationalist even granted the supervenience thesis? No! The reason is that the foundationalist may employ a similar strategy by amending principle (F) so that it is self-justifying by simply picking the property *NB* in such a way that (F) has that property or by adding reference to the principle within it as follows:

(FSR) *S* is justified in accepting that *p* if either *p* has *NB* or is (FSR).

To be sure, the way in which this principle justifies itself lacks the subtlety of having it turn out that the principle justifies itself as a result of cohering with an evaluation system. (FSR) justifies itself immediately rather than as a result of coherence, but that would hardly be a fair objection to a foundationalist advocating a doctrine of immediately justified basic beliefs. The foundationalist advocating (FSR) is in a position to avoid the surd by answering the question of why we are justified in accepting that *p*, by saying that (FSR) tells us so, and of answering the question of why we are justified in accepting what (FSR) tells us, by saying that (FSR) tells us that we are. We are hardly entitled to complain against a theory built on self-justification on the grounds that it justifies itself, especially if we take it to be a virtue of the competing coherence theory that it tells us that justification results from coherence with a system.

If we are interested, therefore, in arguing that the coherence theory has an advantage in explaining why things are justified that the foundations theory must lack, we must reject the thesis of supervenience and argue for a coherence theory that makes justification independent. Moreover, we must do this in such a way as to show why coherence leads to the doctrine of independence and the foundations theory does not. But how can we accomplish this? What is there about coherence that yields independence?

Coherence and Epistemic Worth

The answer, in brief, is that an adequate account of coherence must involve epistemic notions. The sort of justification required for knowledge is undefeated personal justification based on an evaluation system of the person in question.[7] Personal justification is defined in terms of a comparative notion of reasonableness, of whether it is more reasonable for a person to accept one thing rather than another. This comparative notion is epistemic and, though connected with preference within the keystone loop, depends on whether a person is worthy of her own trust concerning acceptance and preference. Whether she is worthy of her own trust depends on whether she is trustworthy in accepting or preferring what has worth and not accepting or preferring what does not. The notion of personal justification rests, therefore, on the epistemic notion of what is *worth* accepting.

Any definition of coherence that is adequate will remain independent within the loop of epistemic terms. Independence implies irreducibility, though not vice versa, because independence is the denial of supervenience, and, hence, of the thesis that non-epistemic properties are sufficient, with

[7] Keith Lehrer, 'Metaknowledge: Undefeated Justification', first published in 1988, reprinted in Keith Lehrer, *Metamind* (Oxford, 1990), ch. 11; and Keith Lehrer, *Theory of Knowledge*.

a kind of metaphysical necessity, for epistemic ones. I shall, therefore, explain why the assumptions behind the coherence theory I defend are incompatible with supervenience. The crux of the matter is that to know anything, one must accept and prefer to accept a minimal epistemic theory about evidence, and be correct in doing so.

Evidence and Trustworthiness

What does a person have to accept about evidence in order to be justified in what she accepts? Take a standard example. I know that I see a hand. That is something that I am justified in accepting and my justification is not defeated by error. I can meet objections, all of them, in fact, and the way I meet them does not depend on error. Now one obvious objection is that my evidence that I see a hand is deceptive. I must deny this, that is, I must accept that the evidence that I see a hand is not deceptive. Another obvious objection is that I do not have any trustworthy way of telling whether the evidence is deceptive. I must deny this too. I accept I am trustworthy in what I accept about the evidence as well as about what I see, to wit, my hand.[8]

Notice, however, that for me to know that I see a hand it is not sufficient that I accept that the evidence is not deceptive. It is not even sufficient that I accept that I am trustworthy in what I accept about the evidence or, for that matter, that I accept that I am trustworthy in what I accept about what I see. These things that I accept about my trustworthiness must also be true or my justification will be defeated. Corrections of my errors must not destroy my justification, and if the things I accept be errors, my justification will be defeated. What I accept about my trustworthiness in these matters must be correct or my justification will not suffice for knowledge. Coherence with an evaluation system, if it is to yield undefeated justification and,

---

[8] Terry L. Price raises the objection in 'Counterexamples and Prophylactics', *Philosophical Studies*, 74 (1994), 273–82, and my reply is 'Denying Deception: A Reply to Terry Price', *Philosophical Studies*, 74 (1994), 283–90.

hence, knowledge, must involve coherence with what we accept about our trustworthiness, and what we accept about it must also be true. Thus, coherence presupposes the truth of epistemic claims.

I shall assume, without further argument, that a person does not know something unless she accepts that her evidence is non-deceptive and is trustworthy in so doing. I recognize that some externalists have offered analyses that run contrary to this claim, and I have attempted elsewhere to counter these.[9] My basic comment on them is that merely receiving information in some reliable manner does not suffice for the person receiving the information to know. The reason is that the person might have no idea that she has received information that is correct or that she has received it in a trustworthy way. If she receives the information that p but does not know that the information that p is trustworthy or correct, then she does not know that p. To know that the information is trustworthy and correct, she must know that her evidence is not deceptive, that she is trustworthy in accepting what she does.

The Regress or the Loop

This claim might seem to lead to regress. It might seem that in order to know that the information she has received is trustworthy and correct, she must know that her evidence is not deceptive, and to know this she must know something else which gives her this knowledge, and so on *ad infinitum*. The answer is contained in the keystone principles and the keystone loop. My acceptance that I am trustworthy in what I accept is something that I also accept and that justifies acceptance of it in conjunction with other things I accept. The acceptance of my trustworthiness, of my being worthy of my trust concerning what I accept, enables me to infer the following conclusion:

(S) If I accept that p, then it is reasonable for me to accept that p.

[9] Keith Lehrer, *Theory of Knowledge*, ch. 8.

Though (S) does not justify itself, it does play a role in the justification of itself together with the other things that I accept. In short, there is a minimal theory about my being trustworthy concerning what I accept and prefer which, together with the things I accept and prefer, converts the raw stuff of acceptance and preference into the constructive materials of knowledge.

Now, this argument might appear simply to generate a principle of supervenience rather than supporting independence, namely, the principle (S) itself. This is not a principle of supervenience, however. The first reason is that (S) is a contingent truth which does hold in other possible worlds and not a necessary truth. Whether it is true depends on what I am actually like, and there is no necessity in that. Nevertheless, a defender of supervenience might insist that if we add the general features, G, about me which would make S true then we would obtain a necessary truth, namely,

> (SG) If I accept that p and I have G, then it is reasonable for me to accept that p.

Put in this way, however, it is apparent that the supervenience claim depends on whether G can be filled in without using epistemic notions. I claim that it cannot be. To see why not, consider the principle

> (At) I am trustworthy in what I accept,

which implies acceptance is more worthy of my trust than non-acceptance. It is normative and epistemic. That observation does not by itself defeat the supervenience claim, for we have yet to show that my trustworthiness does not supervene on non-epistemic properties. How can we show that?

Remember the keystone loop, which circles around my being trustworthy for myself in the same way that it circled around my being worthy of my trust. I am trustworthy in what I accept only if I can tell whether I am trustworthy or not. I must be able to tell whether I am trustworthy or not about something in order to be trustworthy about it. I must accept that I am trustworthy when I am and not accept that I am trustworthy when I am not, at least a trustworthy amount of the time. I must, for example, accept that I am trustworthy in certain kinds of memory beliefs, clear and confident ones, and not trustworthy in others, uncertain and obscure ones, in order to be trustworthy in what I accept about what I remember. The same is true of perception. If I cannot tell when I am trustworthy in what I recall and when not, if I cannot tell when I am trustworthy in what I perceive and when not, then I am not trustworthy in these matters.

The Absurdity of Naturalism

The foregoing observations may be reinforced with a very simple argument. Let us assume, for the purpose of reducing the assumption to absurdity, that justification results from some naturalized coherence relation, n-coherence, to a background evaluation system. Assume that something n-coheres with the things that I accept. Could it follow from such coherence that I am justified in accepting something? Suppose that even I do not think the things I accept are worth accepting. Why should n-coherence with things that I accept, but do not think are worth accepting, justify me in accepting anything? Suppose that I accept that the things I accept are worth accepting. Would it follow from n-coherence with such a system that I am justified in accepting something?

Some kind of justification might result from such n-coherence, but it would be a subjective justification based entirely on what *I* accept about epistemic and factual matters.[10] If I am wrong in what I accept about either of these matters,

---

[10] This naturalized and subjectivized notion of justification is not the same notion as that of personal justification incorporated in the accounts of undefeated justification I have used elsewhere. The notion of personal justification is defined in terms of a primitive epistemic notion of comparative reasonableness on the basis of an acceptance system, and that epistemic notion is not reducible by definition to a naturalized relation.

the subjective justification might not survive the correction of my errors and, therefore, might be defeated by them. Thus, undefeated justification, the stuff of which knowledge is made, requires not only that I accept that the things I accept are worth accepting, but that they really are worth accepting. The worth of their acceptance is an epistemic matter that transcends the natural state of acceptance. Coherence that converts into undefeated justification, the refined stuff of knowledge, depends on our correct acceptance of the worth of what we accept.

Truth and the Worth of Acceptance

The crux of the matter is that it is the trustworthiness of my acceptance, which includes the acceptance of it, that is required for the sort of justification that yields knowledge, to wit, undefeated justification. That is why supervenience fails. There is nothing about me, short of my being trustworthy in what I accept, that necessitates that I am trustworthy in what I accept. There is nothing about what I accept, short of it being worth accepting, that necessitates that it is worth accepting. I might be successful in the pursuit of truth, it might even be a consequence of a law of nature that I am successful, but success, even nomologically backed, does not metaphysically necessitate that I am trustworthy in what I accept or that what I accepted was worth accepting. My success might be luck, even if it is a consequence of a law of nature. Such successes might result, even though acceptance of my trustworthiness is no more worthy of my trust than non-acceptance, and the truth not worth accepting in this case.

Unerring success, even that which is a consequence of a law of nature, might fail to reveal to me and others that I or they are worthy of trust. If natural success in attaining truth could vouch for itself, could reveal that it is worthy of our trust, then supervenience would result. But nature is silent about what has worth, about what is worthy of our trust, and about what is justified. She tells us what will be, not what is worthy of being or of being trusted. Nature tells us what will be, but about what is worthy of being, she is silent as a stone.

Possible Worlds, Worth, and Truth

Can we imagine two worlds that are naturalistically the same, except that in one what people accept is worth accepting, but in the other, not? A person in one world will be right about the course of nature exactly when her naturally identical correlate is right about the course of nature. So how can the one be ignorant when the other knows? That is what independence, the denial of supervenience, implies. How can it be true? Of course, if the person in one world has some idea that her evidence is trustworthy and that she is trustworthy in what she accepts upon it while the other does not, there is an important difference between the two. One understands the epistemic merits of her position, and the other does not. With such a distinction, where one takes her evidence to be worthy of her trust and the other has no idea of the worth of it, the reason for ascribing knowledge to the one and not to the other is clear enough. But what ideas a person has depends on her nature, so two creatures identical to each other in every natural way cannot differ in their ideas. We do not yet have a refutation of supervenience.

The two people may, however, differ in the truth of their ideas when those ideas refer to something beyond natural phenomena. Suppose both believed in supernatural beings, and one world contained such beings but the other not. One would have true beliefs and the other not, though nature was the same in both worlds. If there is no supernatural, then witchmaking properties do not a witch make, even though, in a world with the supernatural, such properties do make someone a witch.

Let us consider properties less controversial than supernatural ones, to argue for the independence of the epistemic. Let us consider truth. Does truth supervene on naturalistic properties? If the answer is negative, then it becomes plausible to suppose that the answer is negative in the case of epistemic properties as well. Truth is, after all, an objective of justification even if there is more to justification than just the attainment of that objective. How might one argue for the independence of truth? Suppose someone argues that T supervenes on B, where B is the base property and T is truth. This amounts to the claim that

(X) If something is B, then it is T,

and, moreover, that this is a necessary truth.

But suppose that (X) is B. Then

(XT) If (X) is B, then (X) is T.

Thus a necessary condition of (X) is the truth of (X). The point is that (X) says of itself that it is true, though perhaps only indirectly. Does this show that (X) is not necessarily true? Not necessarily, but it allows for an argument against the necessity of (X). It seems that there might be two worlds, one in which (X) is true, one in which it is not, which are otherwise, that is, non-semantically, identical. The reason that (X) is true in one world and not in the other is that there is no truth in the one world but there is in the other. There is nothing absurd in denying the necessary truth of such an (X), or, therefore, of supposing that worlds identical non-semantically might differ semantically.

Self-Reference and Independence

What about modified supervenience, that is, the thesis that if anything is true, then truth supervenes on some base property? The defender of supervenience might argue that if there is any truth in a world, then some proposition of the form of (X) is necessarily true. Is that true? It is not obvious. Consider the claim,

(E) Everything that is true is true.

That seems obviously true to some, but not to others, because it violates restrictions regarding language levels. Maybe (E) is true in some possible worlds but not in others that are otherwise the same but restrict the application of the truth-predicate differently. Consider again,

(L) This sentence refers to itself.

Maybe there are possible worlds that are otherwise identical, such that this sentence is true in one and not the others. In some possible worlds, semantically self-referential sentences are neither true nor false, but in others, those that are less restrictive about truth, it is true. Thus, (E) and (R) are sentences which might or might not be true in a world depending on the semantics of those worlds. Two worlds identical non-semantically might have different semantics, different truth-restrictions, and that explains why they are true in one and not true in the other.

There are some simple connections between worlds without truth and worlds without justification, at least undefeated justification, if truth be a worthy goal of justification, indeed, even one among many. In a truthless world, one might accept things about truth and about trustworthy ways of arriving at truth which would yield subjective justification based on one's evaluation system. But the system would contain errors pertaining to truth, and when they were eliminated, the justification would be defeated. Two worlds that were naturalistically identical but semantically different might, therefore, differ with respect to what a person is justified in accepting, at least in an undefeated way. Even two worlds naturalistically identical, so that both contained truth but differed semantically with the result that (L) was true in one and not the other, might, as a result, yield undefeated justification for the acceptance of (L) in the one world but not in the other.

Fact and Value

Does all this have anything to do with coherence? Only this: the coherence theory, at least as I conceive of it, tells us that justification and knowledge result from coherence with a system of evaluation which resolves epistemic conflict by providing defence against competitors to obtain coherence. The system of evaluation articulates the connections between the epistemic and non-epistemic conditions which together yield coherence, justification, and knowledge. That system represents a world of epistemic value and a world of natural fact. Those two worlds must be coherently joined in a true and trustworthy way to yield the world of knowledge. Knowledge does not supervene on the natural world. Coherence is the glue which bonds the natural world, as we conceive of it, to the world of epistemic value, as we conceive of that. The glue of coherence requires matching surfaces of acceptance and truth to hold fast, but it does not bond across possible worlds. Coherence suffices for our knowledge of our actual world and explains how it suffices. The independence of coherence rests on the keystone loop which transcends the epistemic surd. This independence is, however, only a guarantee of contingency. The task of tying this to autonomy of choice in the keystone loop of our trustworthiness remains before us.

FOR FURTHER READING

On supervenience:

Horgan, Terence, 'From Supervenience to Superdupervenience: Meeting the Demands of a Material World', *Mind*, 102 (1993), 555–86.

Kim, Jaegwon, *Supervenience and Mind* (New York: Cambridge University Press, 1993).

Klagge, James, 'Supervenience: Ontological and Ascriptive', *Australasian Journal of Philosophy*, 66 (1988), 461–70.

Van Cleve, James, 'Epistemic Supervenience and the Circle of Belief', *The Monist*, 68 (1985), 90–104.

On epistemology as an autonomous versus a naturalistic subject:

Alston, William P., 'Two Types of Foundationalism', *Journal of Philosophy*, 73 (1976), 165–85.

Chisholm, Roderick, 'The Status of Epistemic Principles', *Nous*, 24 (1990), 209–15.

Foley, Richard, 'What am I to Believe?', in Steven Wagner and Richard Warner (eds.), *Naturalism: A Critical Appraisal* (Notre Dame, Ind.: University of Notre Dame Press, 1993).

Sosa, Ernest, *Knowledge in Perspective* (New York: Cambridge University Press, 1991).

Van Cleve, James, 'Foundationalism, Epistemic Principles and the Cartesian Circle', *Philosophical Review*, 88 (1979), 55–91.

4

Conflict and Autonomy

In this chapter, we shall turn to the existential thesis, the thesis of the priority of autonomy of choice in the keystone loop of acceptance and preference. Autonomous choice is the point at the centre of the loop. At this point, we must remember the role of metamental ascent in acceptance and preference. What is important to the argument is to recall that the human mind not only contains sensations, thoughts, and desires, it also contains something beyond those states. It contains metamental states of acceptance and preference evaluating first-order beliefs and desires. What is special about human mentality is our capacity for metamental ascent and the conceptually explosive consequences thereof.

Conflict and Ascent

It is metamental activity that enables us to spin, construct, destroy, and respin our web of evaluation. Why is it important? What is the function of metamental ascent? An important function of metamental ascent is the resolution of conflict at the first level. We must resolve conflict among our desires to attain reasonable preference, justified preference, and wisdom. We must resolve conflict among our beliefs for reasonable acceptance, justified preference, and knowledge. The resolution of such conflicts is essential to wisdom and knowledge. But how do we resolve them?

The posing of the question suggests the metamental answer. Metamental ascent is required in order to articulate the alternative patterns that resolve the conflict. The patterns generated by metamental ascent are conceptually explosive because of the multiplicity of alternatives for resolving the conflict. The resolution of conflict requires the rejection of some information carried in first-level beliefs and desires because the resolution of conflict is underdetermined by first-level information. Inspection of beliefs and desires, no matter how thorough, is insufficient to resolve conflict. There is only one way to resolve conflict for the purposes of attaining wisdom and knowledge: higher-order evaluation.

Metamental Ascent

Higher-order strategies generate coherent patterns of acceptance and preference from incoherent patterns of first-order belief and desire. Acceptance and preference, incorporating metamental ascent and evaluation, seek to avoid dominance of doubt and paralysis of the will. Metamental ascent rescues us from both Cartesian scepticism and Buridanian asininity. A problem remains. Conflict arises among higher-order strategies. These must be resolved by autonomous choice.

I shall begin by considering an example of first-order conflict concerning desire. The example will illustrate metamental ascent, the proliferation of alternatives, the rejection of first-order information, and the employment of higher-order strategies. It is a simple example involving the choice of a bottle of wine. The example is in honour of my wife Adrienne Lehrer who early fascinated me with wine and conversation and later with her book, *Wine and Conversation*.[1] This simple example illustrates the problems of conflict resolution in theory and practice, in science and society. It will lead us beyond itself to the higher-order exercise of autonomy.

Wine and Transitivity

The example involves a wine-tasting club. The club has definite rules concerning the tasting of wine. First, it is an

---

[1] (Bloomington, Ind., 1983).

exclusive club, and only the members of the club are al-
lowed to drink the wines belonging to the club. Second,
they wish to enjoy the wine they drink without snobbery.
To this end, they disregard all differences between wines
that they cannot discern with the senses as they enjoy it in
the glass. They purchase and drink all wine in ignorance of
the label, for example, on the grounds that the origin of the
wine is as irrelevant as any other feature that cannot be
tasted, smelled, or seen by attending to wine in the glass.
Finally, it is well known that one member of the club,
Archie, has the most refined sensory powers of anyone in
the group. He can distinguish between wines when no one
else can, and no one can distinguish between wines when
he cannot. Archie is the arch discriminator of wines for the
group.

An Example

Here is the example. Archie is assigned the problem of pur-
chasing a case of wine for the group from their wine merchant, Ms. Ratio. She offers him three wines, A, B, and C.
Archie tastes them. He cannot distinguish between A and
B, nor between B and C, but he can distinguish between A
and C and likes A better. All the wines are the same price.
On the basis of his tasting, Archie rates A and B equally desirable, B and C as equally desirable, but A more desirable
than C, and he conveys this information to Ratio.

Ratio tells him that this creates a problem for her because she does not have the wines in stock and must purchase them from her French wine merchant who will
telephone her on Monday offering her a choice between
two of the wines, she does not know which two, and then
telephone her again on Tuesday to let her know whether
the third wine is available or not. If the third wine is not
available on Tuesday, then she will receive the wine she
chose from the two on Monday; but if the third wine is
available, then she will be able to choose between the wine
chosen on Monday and the third wine offered on Tuesday.

A Problem of Choice

The situation creates a problem because the information offered by Archie could lead to the choice of any one of the wines, including C, when all three are available. Consider the following scenario. On Monday, she must choose between A and B. She tosses a coin, since A and B are equally desirable, and she chooses B over A. On Tuesday, she is offered a choice between B and C. She again tosses a coin, since B and C are equally desirable, and chooses C as the wine to be received by Archie and his club. (Had the coin tosses fallen otherwise, Archie might have received A or B.) The problem, as she sees it, is that Archie will receive C when he might have received A and considers A more desirable than C. Moreover, this results simply because B was available as well as A and C.

Principle of Irrelevance

Technically, having done some philosophy and economics, she might add that the information supplied by Archie leads to choices that violate the principle of the irrelevance of independent alternatives, to wit, that if one were to choose A over C when only those two were available, then one should choose A over C when B is also available. The irrationality of violating this principle is illustrated by an alleged Sydney Morgenbesser story. It goes as follows. Morgenbesser enters a restaurant, and the following dialogue occurs between him and a waitress.

> Morgenbesser: I would like a roll or something. What have you got?
> Waitress: I have a sweet roll or a bagel.
> Morgenbesser: I'll have a sweet roll.
> Waitress: I forgot. We also have onion rolls.
> Morgenbesser: Oh, in that case I'll have a bagel instead.

The humour of the story illustrates the irrationality of violating the principle of the irrelevance of independent alternatives.[2]

Ratio might also note that, were the other members to know that Archie bought wine C for them when A was available and he liked A better than C, they would have a right to complain. Finally, and most critically, the problem is one of conflict in supposing that A and B are equally desirable, that B and C are equally desirable and that A is more desirable than C. That, Ratio notes, is what leads us to the conflicting choices. So, Ratio proposes that Archie supply her with information that will enable her to choose for him and the group in such a way that if both A and C are offered, in whatever order, wine C would not be chosen. What should Archie do?

Archie's Conundrum

Let us consider Archie's situation. First of all, notice that his desires are perfectly rational. Since he cannot tell the difference between A and B, it is reasonable for him to consider A and B equally desirable. Indeed, it would be unreasonable for him to think one more desirable than the other. He is acting for a group in which he is the arch taster, differences he cannot discern no one in the group can, and the group has no interest in differences they cannot discern. It would be unreasonable, therefore, for Archie to infer from the fact that he liked A better than C, that A was more desirable than B, or that B was more desirable than C. For given that one is only interested in differences one can discern with the senses, and one cannot discern any difference between A and B or between B and C, it follows that A and B are equally desirable, as are B and C. At the level of desire, then, there is nothing unreasonable in what Archie told Ratio.

The problem arises when desires are used as the basis of

[2] There is a growing empirical literature suggesting that cases like this are common in the real world. (See, e.g., E. Shafir and A. Tversky, 'Thinking through Uncertainty: Nonconsequential Reasoning and Choice', *Cognitive Psychology*, 24 (1992), 449–74.)

choice. Archie's pattern of desire can generate the choice of any alternative, including C, even if A is available. The situation with Ratio illustrates the further fact that affairs of real life may have the consequence that one cannot first choose between A and C when all three alternatives are available. What Ratio is asking of Archie is that he reflect on his desires to provide further guidance beyond his articulation of reasonable desirabilities as the basis of choice. Notice that the use of Ratio as an intermediary is only heuristic. The problem would not be changed if we suppose that Archie is left to deal with the French wine merchant himself. We may think of Ratio as merely a voice within Archie, the female voice of reason added to the male voice of desire to reach androgynous consensus.

Beyond Desire: Ratio's Advice

Archie must go beyond desire to preference. I used the word *indifference* like the word *preference* to express a higher-order evaluation that, in this case, has as an aim to obtain a ranking that the person, or some surrogate acting benevolently and logically on behalf of the person, can employ for choice. We have reached metamental ascent. Archie must evaluate his first-order desires to articulate higher-order preferences.

Suppose Archie consults Ratio for advice about what his options are. The first-level conflict of desire that must be resolved results from the fact that Archie's first-order desires mandate a choice of A over C when both are available and permit the choice of C over A when B is available as a result of pairwise choice. Thus, Ratio will observe that what is needed is a preference ranking that will ensure that A is chosen over C when both are available. She will, consequently, inform Archie that he must provide her with a ranking of preference and indifference that is coherent, and, in particular, transitive. After doing a little combinatorial logic, she informs him that any one of five rankings will ensure that A is chosen over C.

Representing the rankings by writing an alternative that is preferred to another above it in a list and indifferent alternatives on the same level, the five rankings are as follows:

Preference Rankings

1. Centring	2. Raising	3. Lowering
A	AB	A
B	C	BC
C		

4. Extreme Raising	5. Extreme Lowering
B	A
A	C
C	B

It is easy to see how the five preference rankings result. The original desirabilities contained three bits of information:

Desirability Information

AB	BC	A
		C

The last bit of information concerning desire is conserved in all five of the preference rankings. All ensure that A will be chosen over C when the choice between the wines conforms to the preference rankings. No matter what wines the French merchant offers on Monday and Tuesday, A will be chosen over C. So all five patterns suffice to that end.

This simple problem illustrates the features of conflict resolution mentioned above. First of all, resolution of the conflict requires metamental ascent. Secondly, metamental ascent generates a number of alternative solutions. Thirdly, all of the solutions involve the rejection of some of the original information, in this case, at least one bit of information about desirabilities. Fourthly, the choice among the alternative solutions is underdetermined by the first-level information. Finally, as we shall see, the resolution of the conflict requires higher-order strategies for choosing among the solutions.

Centring

The standard solution to problems of failure of transitivity of indifference is to choose ranking one, centring. One reason for this is a formal method proposed by Luce for converting intransitive patterns of desire into transitive patterns of preference which yields centring as the pattern of preference.[3] Wagner and I showed, however, that there are also formal methods, very similar to the one proposed by Luce, that convert intransitive patterns of desire into transitive patterns of preference yielding patterns two or three, raising or lowering.[4] So there does not seem to be any purely formal reason for selecting centring over raising or lowering.

Another reason for taking centring as the solution to such problems is that it is inferred that there must be some indiscernible difference between A and B and between B and C that explains why A is more desirable than C and, therefore, that this indiscernible difference between A and B and between B and C shows that A is better than B and that B is better than C. However, the special features of the example exclude this line of reasoning. In this case, only discernible differences matter to the wine-tasting group and, therefore, indiscernible differences are not a legitimate basis for preference. There is no discernible difference between A and B or between B and C.

Conservation

The conclusion is that first-level information underdetermines the choice between the alternatives generated meta-

[3] Duncan Luce, 'Semi-Orders and a Theory of Utility Discrimination', *Econometrica*, 24 (1956), 178–91.

[4] Keith Lehrer and Carl Wagner, 'Intransitive Indifference: The Semi-Order Problem', *Synthese*, 65 (1985), 249–56.

mentally. What should Archie do? He must ascend to a
higher level and ask what strategy is appropriate for choice
One higher-order strategy is to conserve as much of the original information as possible. Let us call this the *conservation
principle*. This principle argues against choosing centring
extreme raising and extreme lowering, because they conserve less of the original information than the other two
rankings of raising or lowering. Each of these three rankings conserves only one bit of the original information and
rejects two bits. Raising and lowering conserve two bits of
original information each, the equal desirability of A and B
or of B and C together with desirability of A over C.

Rejection and Selection

One need not find the principle of the conservation of information decisive, but application of the principle nar-
rows the choice to two alternatives, raising and lowering
How should Archie choose between these two?

Many find a *principle of rejection* a plausible strategy. This
principle tells us that if something is less desirable than another alternative and nothing is less desirable than it, then
one should reject it, that is, prefer the other alternatives
Alternative C is less desirable than A and nothing is less
desirable than C, so both A and B are preferred to it. If we
combine the principle of the conservation of information
with the principle of rejection, we select raising and
Archie's problem is solved.

Others, however, find a *principle of selection* attractive
This principle tells us that if something is more desirable
than something else and nothing is more desirable than it
then one should select it, that is, prefer it to the other alternatives. This principle would lead to the choice of lowering.

Symmetry

Must one accept either lowering or raising? We noted some
bad arguments for accepting centring, but there is, perhaps
a good argument. Alternative B is, so to speak, a wild card

The ranking of A over C is justified by the first-order information that A is more desirable than C, which leaves it completely open where B should be ranked. A *principle of symmetry* would tell us to treat B symmetrically with respect to A and C and, therefore, that B should be neither rejected nor selected. More abstractly, the principle would tell us that if a first alternative is ranked above a second, then any third alternative that is no less desirable than the first and no less desirable than the second should be ranked between them.

(It should be noted finally that if the principle of the conservation of information is maintained and the principles of rejection, selection, and symmetry all rejected, a sixth alternative emerges, namely, indifference between A, B, and C. This ranking conserves two bits of the original information but not the salient information that A is more desirable than C.)

Priority of Autonomy

What is the conclusion? It is a defence of the existential thesis of the priority of autonomy. Why? Metamental ascent generates a number of alternatives each of which rejects some information. Selection of an alternative is underdetermined by the first-level information and depends on higher-order principles. But there is conflict between higher-order principles as well. Suppose, for example, that Archie finds raising, R, equally desirable as centring, C, and also finds lowering, L, equally desirable as centring. This is because, though raising and lowering satisfy the principle of the conservation of information and the principles of rejection and selection respectively, centring satisfies the principle of symmetry. Yet when Archie compares raising and lowering, he finds raising more desirable because, if C is not to be treated symmetrically with respect to R and L, he thinks it is more desirable to reject L by the principle of rejection than to select R by the principle of selection. The result is that transitivity fails at the higher level when Archie is choosing between rankings, just as it failed at the first level when Archie was choosing between wines.

Higher-Level Conflict

Here is the higher-level problem. The desirability ranking is as follows:

$$RC \quad CL \quad R$$
$$L$$

The three main preference rankings to choose from are as follows:

Raising, R	Centring, C	Lowering, L
RC	R	R
L	C	LC
	L	

But notice that the choice of any one of the three is problematic. If Archie chooses lowering, L, then he is using L when he considers using R more desirable than using L. That is paradoxical. If, as seems most reasonable initially, he chooses raising, R, that being the only alternative he considers more desirable than any other, then he is indifferent between R and C. In that case, however, he should be indifferent between using R and using C to solve his higher-order problem. So suppose he uses centring, C. In that case, he is using C when he prefers using R to using C to solve his higher-order problem by centring, C. That is again paradoxical. This suggests that he should prefer R over both L and C, but then he is using lowering, L, when he considers R more desirable than L and, indeed, prefers using R to using L to solve his higher-order problem. We have cycled around in paradox attempting to solve the higher-order problem by appeal to a principle, whether it be raising, centring, or lowering.

The problem of conflict resolution can arise at any higher level concerning strategies, methods, or principles we might use to resolve conflict at the first level. The attempt to use a principle to resolve higher-order conflict leads to paradox. Appeal to a higher-order evaluation is necessary to resolve conflict, but there is no level of metamental ascent that yields a principle which ensures that further evaluation is superfluous in order to resolve conflict. At any level of evaluation, conflict may again emerge, and the attempt to use a principle to resolve higher-order conflict will lead to paradox.

Archie gains something as a result of his metamental cogitation, none the less. He articulates with the help of Ms. Ratio a set of preference rankings any one of which suffices to resolve his conflict. He need only exercise his autonomy and choose one of the rankings to obtain transitivity and resolve the conflict. He should not think, however, that his choice is guided by a principle sufficient to resolve higher-order conflict should it arise.

Features of Optionality and Conflict Resolution

The proliferation of alternatives reveals the way in which optionality may be expanded by higher-order reflection. You might find the higher order perplexing. I suggest it is the stuff of which autonomy is made. Archie is not locked into his first-order perplexity. Ratio frees him from first-order entrenchment by metamental ascent. These are the features required to resolve first-order conflict by metamental ascent: rejection of first-order information, expansion of the set of alternatives, and autonomous choice. The process enhances optionality. Conflict is resolved by metamental ascent and the exercise of autonomy.

Metamental ascent combined with the exercise of autonomy yields a unified theory of reason, justification, knowledge, and wisdom. We can imagine creatures driven by first-order belief and desire from input to output in thought and action. Philosophers sometimes write as though we were such creatures, neglecting their own metamental reflections on their first-order beliefs and desires in a moment of philosophical absent-mindedness. Without metamental processing we would be blind to the existence of our own beliefs and desires. Beliefs and desires might lead to other beliefs and desires, and those to thought and action, without metamental ascent, but then we would be ignorant of our beliefs and desires. They would lie beyond our evaluation and we would be blindly driven by them. In fact, we are not blind but informed, and we not driven but autonomous. Conflict provokes metamental ascent and reveals the ubiquity of it in the evaluation of acceptance and preference. That is the conclusion I draw, and now the conclusion draws me.

Acceptance

What is the state of acceptance? It is a state that has a certain functional role in reasoning, thought, and action. The role is the one that typically arises from reflectively judging that something is the case, but it may arise from default processing of information rather than from conscious reflection. I may reflectively judge that the door is open and accept as a result that the door is open. Or I may see that the door is open and accept unreflectively that the door is open. The consequences of what I think, infer, and do will be the same no matter which way my acceptance comes about.

When the information that I receive and thus minimally believe, does not produce conflict, I accept the information, I accept what I believe. In this simple case, there may be a correspondence between belief and acceptance. In the case of conflict, metamental ascent will normally result in the rejection of some first-order information or belief to resolve the conflict, the consideration of alternatives beyond what I believe, and this will break the correspondence between what is believed and what is accepted. Whether acceptance results from routine processing of first-order belief or the more complicated procedures of conflict resolution, acceptance is a metamental state produced by the higher-order evaluation, whether routine or reflective.

Preference

Returning from acceptance to preference yields a parallel structure. Without conflict, the default processing of desire yields preference. Preference is a state with a functional role in thought, reasoning, and action. The functional state is the one that characteristically arises when one reflectively decides to choose one thing rather than another, though it may arise without reflection. I desire to drink some water sitting before me rather than going thirsty. I may decide upon reflection to drink the water rather than going thirsty and prefer drinking the water to going thirsty in this way. Or I may form the preference unreflectively. In the simple case, I prefer drinking to going thirsty without reflecting on the matter. The consequences in terms of what I think, infer, or do will be the same no matter how the preference arises.

When there is no conflict between desires, there may be an exact correspondence between desire and preference, while in the case of conflict, metamental ascent will result in the rejection of some first-order desire and consideration of some alternative beyond what is desired to resolve the conflict. The correspondence between desire and preference will be broken. Whether preference arises in a routine manner or from more complicated procedures of conflict resolution, preference is the result of metamental evaluation.

Reason and Autonomy

Here is my model of diachronic reason turning around the central point of autonomy. There are first-order states which I have referred to as beliefs and desires. I have exercised some linguistic licence in this usage to which I now wish to admit. What I have been calling belief is our characteristic attitude toward information that we receive from our senses and other people. We receive information from these sources and, in a sense, initially believe what they tell us. This is a minimal notion of belief. Such information, such belief, may, however, be accepted or rejected on the basis of background information, of an evaluation system we already have.

The default mode is to accept the received belief. Similarly, the default mode is to prefer the satisfaction of desire. In the default mode, acceptance of belief or preference for the satisfaction of the desire goes unnoticed. The process of evaluation seems automatic and is invisible. Acceptance and preference are driven by an objective of accepting what is worth accepting and preferring what is worth preferring which takes us beyond the mere presence of belief and desire to an evaluation of it.

Belief and Transitivity

When there is conflict between a belief and other beliefs or between a desire and other desires, the role of metamental ascent and higher-order evaluation becomes blatant. We are then faced with the features of conflict resolution encountered in the wine example. We encounter examples of exactly the same logical structure concerning beliefs as we have considered concerning desires. Suppose I have a balance scale and three objects, A, B, and C. I see that A and B are equal in weight and that B and C are equal in weight, for they balance each other. Nevertheless, I see that A is heavier than C. I might accept all three bits of information. Metamental ascent would yield a number of alternatives with the same formal structure as the wine case, and, in this instance, the natural strategy for most people would be centring, that is, to accept that A is heavier than B, that B is heavier than C and that A is heavier than C, even though this strategy involves the rejection of two bits of original information. The reason for adopting this strategy, however, is because one accepts a background theory implying that there is a hidden difference between A and B and between B and C that explains the sensory information. That theory incorporates a higher-order principle.

The appeal to a higher-order strategy is essential because first-order information must be insufficient to resolve the conflict. One might, of course, resolve a certain level of conflict by finding a more sensitive measuring device, but any measuring device has a least measure, a measure beyond which further differences will not be noticed. There are just noticeable differences for measuring devices as well as for us. So the ultimate resolution of conflict must be the result of metamental ascent and the autonomous choice of higher-level strategies.

To understand the role of autonomy, consider first the simplest example of conflict, a minimally inconsistent set of beliefs, belief that p_1, belief that p_2, and belief that p_3, such that any pair of the beliefs is consistent. How are we to resolve the conflict? Metamental ascent reveals four salient strategies respecting the objective of conserving belief: the acceptance of p_1 and p_2, the acceptance of p_2 and p_3, the acceptance of p_1 and p_3, or the acceptance of all three.

The last alternative, the acceptance of an inconsistent set, has the disadvantage of guaranteeing the acceptance of something false but has the advantage of conserving the most original information. The other three strategies all involve the rejection of at least some first-level information but allow the possibility, at least, of accepting only truths. We already confront the role of autonomy when we consider whether or not it is worth accepting all three beliefs when it is impossible to accept only truths. But the role of autonomy becomes more apparent at the level of methods of acceptance and preference, as we have seen above, and this brings us into the keystone loop in a new way.

We have noted that the problem of conflict resolution can arise at any higher level concerning the principles of conflict resolution themselves. Moreover, the appeal to such principles, for example, raising, centring, and lowering, to resolve conflict among them leads to paradox. We cannot count on a principle to solve the problem. We must exercise our autonomy to resolve the conflict as it arises. We must ultimately place our trust in ourselves rather than in a principle. It is our trustworthiness in acceptance, preference, and reasoning that makes the resolution of conflict by autonomous choice reasonable.

The Role of Autonomy

We must choose to resolve conflict and be personally justified in preferring what we do for the preference to be a wise one. But must the choice be autonomous as the existential thesis tells us? I wish to defend a positive answer. My preference for the principle of resolving conflict and acceptance of the merit of the principle depend on the assumption that I am worthy of my trust in my preferences and acceptances. The assumption that I am not autonomous in my preferences is, however, a competitor to the preference. This is not because it is an opposing preference but because it is more reasonable for me to prefer what I do on the assumption that it is true that I am autonomous in my preference than on the assumption that this false. The explanation is that I am more worthy of my trust concerning my preference if I am autonomous in my preference than if I am not. The assumption that I am not autonomous is, therefore, a competitor for any preference and, indirectly, for any acceptance as well.

The preceding argument amounts to the claim that preference and acceptance have the claim that I am not autonomous as a competitor. This claim is, in other words, an objection that must be met by my evaluation system to yield personally justified preferences and acceptances which convert, when undefeated, to wisdom and knowledge. To substantiate the claim concerning autonomy, we shall need an analysis of autonomy to which I shall soon turn.

An Objection

We can, however, confront an objection to the alleged competitor in a preliminary manner with only the tool of intuition to guide us. Someone might reply that a person might consider herself to lack autonomy but to be worthy of her trust, none the less, and, therefore, she can be personally justified in what she prefers and accepts. In the terminology of our theory, this is an attempt to neutralize the competitor to my preference. The competitor is:

(C) I am not autonomous in what I prefer,

which is neutralized by conjoining to it the neutralizer:

(N) I am worthy of my trust concerning what I prefer anyway.

Now the question is whether (N) is a successful neutralizer to the objection (C). I cannot deny that there are people, some very intelligent people among them, for whom (N) would successfully neutralize (C). Perhaps Spinoza was among them. Such people have a theory within their acceptance systems explaining why they do not need to be autonomous to be worthy of their own trust. For example, one might accept that, though everything one accepts and prefers results from a system of necessity, the system of necessity is worthy of trust.

My claim is that such neutralization of the objection that a person is not autonomous, though successful for personal justification, will be defeated by errors within the evaluation system if, in fact, the person is not autonomous. I am now, I admit, opposing my evaluation system, at least that part of it concerned with issues of autonomy, against many influential philosophers, and I do so with trepidation. Nevertheless, the matter strikes me as a clear one.

The Need for Autonomy

Let me put the matter in the first person, candidly making the appeal to my evaluation system as explicit as possible. I cannot be worthy of my trust if I am not autonomous because, if the evaluations I make are imposed or fortuitous, I have no way of telling whether what I evaluate as worth accepting or preferring is worth accepting or preferring.

Suppose I am powerless and must accept what I am told to accept, prefer what I am told to prefer. I might, doing what I am told, reach some goals I seek, but I am not worthy of my trust because I am helpless. I am not the author of these preferences and acceptances. Someone, something, or nothing is, but I am not, and that is the difficulty.

Suppose I accept that I am not autonomous. How can I begin the sequence of self-trust, how can I trust myself, how can I trust myself in what I accept and prefer, when I am helpless and cannot help doing what I do, accepting what I do, preferring what I do, evaluating as I do? If I do not trust myself, how can I be worthy of my trust? The crux is this. When I evaluate the worth of things, I must assume that my evaluation is autonomous for me to be the author of those evaluations, for them to be mine, and, therefore, for me to be worthy of my trust.

Autonomy Analysed

We must be autonomous to be worthy of our trust. But what is autonomy? We shall find the loop of reference contained in the answer. Kant thought that autonomous action required that the agent be author of the law, maxim, or principle of the action.[5] The choice of principle may need to be autonomous, but not every autonomous choice need be principled. If there is, for example, an autonomous choice of principles, that choice may not be itself a choice of principle. Kant's requirement places too great an emphasis on principle. Action and preference can be autonomous and unprincipled, for example, when an agent wants to act spontaneously and succeeds. Is autonomy just doing what we want, then?

Addiction and Desire

Autonomy is not just doing what we want. There are two reasons. One is that we may do what we want when we

[5] Immanuel Kant, *Foundations of the Metaphysics of Morals* (1785), 1st edn. trans. and intro. by Lewis White Beck (Indianapolis, Ind., 1975), sect. 2.

would prefer not to want to do what we want to do. There may be a conflict, as Frankfurt has noted, between a first-order desire and a higher-order preference.[6] If I am addicted to some substance, activity, or person, I may find myself doing what I want to do but prefer not to want to do what I want to do. It is not that I do not want to do what I do; I want to do what I do, but I would prefer not to want to. The ingestion or injection of some substance that I want because I am physically and/or psychologically addicted to it may be an example, when I consider my addictions and the use of the substance harmful and destructive. It is not that I do not want to use the drug. I do want to use it. I want very badly to use it and may go to a great deal of effort to obtain the drug to use. It is just that I prefer not to be addicted and not to want to use the drug that I, in fact, use and want to use.

Or suppose I am addicted to exercise, to bicycling, for example. I bicycle all the time at the expense of my work and relations to other people. Perhaps it is because I am a champion bicyclist, my life is failing in many ways, I am failing in many ways, and only bicycling makes me feel like a winner rather than a failure. So I want to bicycle, and I do bicycle. But I would prefer to have the strength of character to face the problems in my life and deal with those problems rather than just wanting to bicycle all the time.

Or take a third case. I am in love with a woman. She was in love with me at one time but has rejected me. When she loved me, it was wonderful. She and her love for me had a magical effect on me. I felt valued and valuable, desired and desirable, and these feelings filled me with further feelings of confidence and strength. She has rejected me, and I no longer feel valuable, desirable, confident, and

---

[6] Harry Frankfurt, 'Freedom of the Will and the Concept of a Person', *Journal of Philosophy*, 68 (1971), 5–20. See also Richard Jeffrey, 'Preferences among Preferences', *Journal of Philosophy*, 71 (1974), 377–91; Keith Lehrer, 'Preferences, Conditionals and Freedom', ch. 3 of Keith Lehrer, *Metamind* (Oxford, 1990); and Wright Neely, 'Freedom and Desire', *Philosophical Review*, 83 (1974), 32–54.

strong, but, instead, worthless, undesirable, unsure, and weak. I feel awful, and I want her love back. I want to get her to love me again. I want to phone her. But I know that she will not love me again and phoning her will only make me feel worse. But I want to phone her. So I phone her because I want to phone her but preferring not to want to phone her. My phoning her feels compelled and is not autonomous.

All of these examples are ones in which I do what I want but do not act autonomously nor do I feel that I do. Let us refer to this as the internal problem, because the actions are and feel compelled by internal states or conditions.

External Manipulation

The second problem for autonomy arises when, though I do what I want, I do not act autonomously because my wanting what I do is manipulated by another. One extreme example is that of responding to a post-hypnotic suggestion. It is suggested to me under hypnosis that I will wash my hands when the bell rings at three o'clock. When the bell rings, I want to wash my hands and do so. I do not know why I want to do this. The question does not occur to me.

There are other crueller cases in which I am brainwashed, and more extraordinary cases in which my brain is mechanically manipulated, or more familiar ones in which I respond to subtle manipulation that leads me to want to buy something of a certain brand without knowing why. Or I may simply be in a situation where the only thing that I want is to please another no matter how contrary to my own real interests this may be. In all of these cases, I may do what I want but still not act autonomously because what I want to do is manipulated by another person. Let us call this the manipulation problem.

Preference and Desire

The solution to the first problem is to require that I do something, not because I want to do it, but because I prefer to satisfy the desire to do it. We have distinguished desire from preference. Preference involves transcendence beyond the first level of desire to a higher or metamental level of evaluation.[7] The importance of the higher level is that it is necessary for freedom from the bondage of first-order desire, however delicious such bondage may at times be.

Desires, like their epistemic cousins, beliefs, arise in us more or less automatically without our bidding and sometimes in opposition to our wishes. I am content working on a philosophical paper, feeling free in philosophical reflection, and then a familiar fragrance catches my nose, a form my eyes, and I am absorbed in desire, my reflective tranquillity dissolved in the immediacy of desire. The desire is there. I did not invite it or wish it, but there it is. Desire is like that. Preference results when I resolve the conflict, one way or another, between the desire for philosophy and desire for the other. Preference is transcendence above the first-order motivations of desire. It is a higher level.

Higher-Order Preferences

Preference for satisfying desire may solve the internal compulsion problem but does not solve the external manipulation problem. Second-order, third-order, and nth-order preferences may all be externally manipulated. A preference for a desire and even a preference for that preference and so on, however iterated, still does not guarantee that one is autonomous.

One might think that if I have a preference for doing A, a preference for having that preference, a preference for having that preference, and so on, then I am autonomous. But that is false. The whole infinite sequence of preferences for preferences might be generated by another. Autonomy requires not just that I prefer my preference but that I be the author of that preference, that my preference be grounded in me and not in another.

[7] Keith Lehrer, *Metamind*, Introduction.

The Power Preference

What does it mean for me to be the author of my preferences? It means that I have the preferences that I do because I prefer to have those preferences. In short, there is a special preference, a kind of power preference, to have just the preference structure I do have concerning my preference that p which is essential to my autonomy. It is the preference described by (PP) as follows:

> (PP) I have the preference structure concerning my preference that p because I prefer to have that preference structure concerning my preference that p.

Suppose my preference that p is a preference that I do A, and, hence, my preference to do A. The preference structure contains a first-order preference for doing A and higher-order preferences so far as they exist pertaining to the preference to do A. Thus, for example, I might have a first-level preference to do A, a second-level preference for that preference concerning A, and so forth. My preference, (PP), for this preference structure, I call the *power preference*, because it empowers me and makes me autonomous.

The preference structure might be integrated in the sense that I prefer to do A all the way up the preference structure. I prefer to do A, prefer to have that preference, prefer to have the preference to have that preference, and so on. It would, however, be a mistake to require integration of the preference structure, even if it only extended up a couple of levels. It is natural to seek integration of one's preference structure for the sake of consistency between levels. But consistency is not everything. I may prefer conflict between levels as an expression of a moral conflict I wish to respect. Suppose, for example, that I have an extreme moral conflict about whether to prefer doing A or B when I cannot do both. Suppose each choice is miserable, though I must choose to avoid a worse. (Sophie's Choice is an example.) Though I prefer to do A, the moral conflict is unresolved, and I may, out of moral concern, prefer to keep it unresolved. I prefer to do *A* while at the same time I prefer not to have that preference because of the moral misery of the choice. I can prefer to have the preference structure that I have concerning *A*, including my preference to do *A* and my preference not to have that preference. Thus, I may be autonomous in my preference to do *A* even though my preference structure remains unintegrated as an expression of my moral conflict. Moreover, the conflict need not be moral to remain expressed in conflict between levels. The advantage of analysing autonomy in terms of a level, ambiguous power preference is that it allows us to combine autonomy with conflict between levels of preference.

The Power Preference Loop and Manipulation

The power preference loops back onto itself because it is itself part of my preference structure with respect to doing *A*. Moreover, it is a preference that I have because I prefer to have it. The force of *because* is explanatory. The power preference explains why I have the preferences I have concerning *A*. It is a kind of first mover of preference. The analysis solves the external manipulation problem because the power preference precludes external manipulation. If I have the preference structure that I do because I prefer to have it, then it cannot be the case that the preferences of it are imposed by another, nor, for that matter, can they be fortuitous.

If I prefer something, and, moreover, prefer to prefer it, and so forth, all those preferences may be produced by another or they might arise in me fortuitously. But if we add the power preference, which refers to all levels of preference and to itself as well, we preclude external manipulation by adding the requirement that this preference explain why I have the preference structure I do, that is, when we add that I have the preference structure because I prefer to have it. If I am externally manipulated by another who creates a preference structure in me, whatever it might be, I do not have the preference structure I do because I prefer to have it, but because the manipulator makes me have it. If I have it because I prefer to have it, then it follows that I am not manipulated into having that preference structure by some external manipulator. I, not the other, am the author of the preference.

Autonomy and the Liar

The self-referential feature of the power preference implies that the truth of the statement that I have the power prefer-ence is not externally grounded in semantic terms. The truth of the statement that I have this preference is not se-mantically grounded in anything external to the preference itself. The ungroundedness of some statements leads to the paradoxes of the liar,

This sentence is false,

and the oddity of the truth-teller,

This sentence is true.

But this feature of ungroundedness is precisely what is de-sired in analysis of autonomy.

Moreover, the analysis enables us to give an account of autonomy without appeal to the notion of the self as cause. The theory of the self as cause, though not without plausi-bility, for I do seem to be the cause of my autonomous pref-erences and actions, leaves us with an unexplained notion of the self as cause. The power preference, by contrast, pro-vides us with an explanation of what makes me the cause of my preferences in a structure, namely, that I have the preferences because I prefer to have them.

The Point of Autonomy

Autonomous preference loops back onto itself to provide us with the point of power at the centre of the keystone loop. From that point of autonomous preference, we find the autonomous self evaluating belief and desire to accept what is worth accepting and prefer what is worth preferring. The power preference loops back onto itself at the centre to make us worthy of our trust concerning what we accept and prefer. As a result, we are reasonable concerning what we accept and prefer. We are, then, reasonable in preferring what we do autonomously, including what we prefer to accept. Autonomous preference is the point of power at the centre of the keystone loop. It enables us to be trustworthy in what we accept and prefer and, ultimately, to obtain knowledge and wisdom from undefeated justification based on autonomous evaluation. Autonomy is the point of the keystone loop.

FOR FURTHER READING

On preference and autonomy:

Ekstrom, Laura Waddell, 'A Coherence Theory of Autonomy', *Philosophy and Phenomenological Research*, 53 (1993), 599–616.

Frankfurt, Harry, 'Freedom of the Will and the Concept of a Person', *Journal of Philosophy*, 68 (1971), 5–20.

Lehrer, Keith, 'Metamind, Autonomy and Materialism', *Grazer Philosophische Studien*, 40 (1991), 1–11.

—— 'Preferences, Conditionals and Freedom', reprinted in Keith Lehrer, *Metamind* (Oxford: Clarendon Press, 1990), ch. 3.

Mele, Alfred, 'Akrasia, Self-Control, and Second-Order Desires', *Nous*, 26 (1992), 281–302.

Neely, Wright, 'Freedom and Desire', *Philosophical Review*, 83 (1974), 32–54.

Swanton, Christine, *Freedom: A Coherence Theory* (Indianapolis, Ind.: Hackett Publishing Co., 1992).

Thalberg, I., 'Hierarchical Analyses of Unfree Action', *Canadian Journal of Philosophy*, 8 (1978), 211–26.

Watson, Gary, 'Free Agency', *Journal of Philosophy*, 72 (1975), 205–20.

Zimmerman, David, 'Hierarchical Motivation and Freedom of the Will', *Pacific Philosophical Quarterly*, 62 (1981), 354–68.

On preference and rationality:

Grofman, Bernard, and Carole Uhlaner, 'Metapreferences and the

Reasons for Stability in Social Choice', *Theory and Decision*, 19 (1985), 31–50.

Jeffrey, Richard, *The Logic of Decision* (New York: McGraw-Hill, 1965).

MacIntosh, Duncan, 'Preference Revision and the Paradoxes of Instrumental Rationality', *Canadian Journal of Philosophy*, 22 (1992), 503–29.

5

Love and Transcendence

We have before us an account of reason, knowledge, wisdom and autonomy connected within the keystone loop of self-trust. We need to open the loop beyond the self to include others, and that will be the concern of the next two chapters. The amalgamation of others into the keystone loop of acceptance and preference depends on the relationship between ourselves and others. To understand the amalgamation, we must understand the relations, especially those that lead to our acceptance and preference for what others accept and prefer and their reciprocation. There is a dramatic play within such relations, as any wise person knows. Let us begin with the romantic star of the show. We shall consider love in this chapter and consider how the transcendence from desire to autonomous preference takes us beyond the love of bondage to autonomous love.

Love and Autonomy

People want to love others and to be autonomous. There is conflict between love and autonomy, according to Sartre, that leads him to conclude that others are hell.[1] We did not, however, need Sartre to inform us that there are tensions between love and autonomy. But why should there be conflict? We might wish to possess the freedom of another like a thing when we love, as Sartre suggests,[2] but why should

---

[1] Jean-Paul Sartre, *Being and Nothingness*, trans. Hazel E. Barnes (New York, 1956), Pt. 3, ch. III, sect. 1. See also Pt. 4, ch. I, pp. 522 ff.

[2] Ibid., Pt. 3, ch. III, sect. 1, pp. 366-7.

love involve that desire for possession of the other's freedom? And why should the desire to be autonomous interfere with loving another? What is there about love and autonomy that produces the strife? Is there no way that we can love and be autonomous? Is there no way that we can love and respect the autonomy of the other? To answer these questions we shall have to understand the structure of love.

Extreme Love

What is love?[3] Love comes in many flavours. Let us consider one form of love which is the basis of much of the world's romantic literature. I shall call it extreme love. It arises within a nexus of sexual desire, and may be characterized in terms of sexual desire. Desire is exquisite in love. The desire to satisfy the sexual desires of another is one of the most delicious forms of desire. It is often thought that some trait of another is the basis of love, and so it may be, but desire is salient. Moreover, as has oft been noticed philosophically and in more intimate ways, sexual love is often aroused by the desire of one person, which arouses the desire of the other, and so on into a spiral of mutual desire.[4] Moreover, satisfying the desire of the other for pleasure is itself a pleasure, as is receiving the pleasure of satisfaction. Those who desire and respond to the satisfaction of their desires with pleasure are seductive lovers. The pleasure of satisfying the desires of another becomes the structure of extreme love and defines it.

Extreme love results when the lover and the loved one are united in each desiring the satisfaction of the desires of the other, until the one dominant desire of each is the satisfaction of the desires of the other. This pattern of desire, I

[3] See articles on love in Peter A. French, Theodore E. Uehling, and Howard K. Wettstein (eds.), *Midwest Studies in Philosophy*, 10 (1986), 399–412, 413–30. See also Ronald De Sousa, *The Rationality of Emotion* (Cambridge, Mass., 1987).

[4] Thomas Nagel, 'Sexual Perversion', *Journal of Philosophy*, 65 (1969), 5–17.

think, accounts for the magic of extreme love and the conflict with autonomy. But first the magic.

Matthew and Rachel are about to become lovers. He noticed her in the lecture hall, and afterward she walked up
to him at the reception and introduced herself. They knew
after a short time that they were to go somewhere and become lovers, but there was the problem of getting from
where they were to somewhere. As conversations drifted
from here to there, Rachel became animated and smiled her
desire at Matthew who immediately succumbed to the
power of it. The desire in her smile was delicious and filled
him with desire—or had the desire in his voice evoked the
desire she had smiled at him? Who knows? And what does
it matter? They will find their way from where they are so
that they can enjoy their desires, each enjoying his or her
own desire for the other and each enjoying the desire of the
other for the other, and, in a refinement of desire, each desiring the desire of the other. As they find their way from
where they are to somewhere where they can make love,
each will experience the miracle of the pleasure of satisfying the other and the pleasure of the other at satisfying
their desire. Pleasure given will be pleasure received, satisfying the desire of the other will become desired itself, and
each will experience the magic of finding satisfaction in
giving satisfaction and, consequently, the desire of the
other for desires in the other that one may satisfy.

The essence of extreme love is a desire to satisfy the desires of the other. Desire to satisfy the desires of the other
produces a natural kind of magic. Whatever happens, you
get what you desire with the bonus of its being desired. If
you get what you desire, she will desire that you do and
thus get what she desires, as you, getting what you desire,
also get the bonus of it being what she desires. If, on the
other hand, she gets what she desires, that is what you desire, and she then gets what she desires with the bonus of it
being what you desire. Your desire and her desire become
entwined as a metaphor for other entwinings, and that is
the magic of it.

The extension of this pattern of desire from sex to other matters is almost invisible. He gives her roses. She never liked roses, but in the roses she smells his desire for her to like roses. She desires the roses, sniffing his desire in them. She makes him popcorn, which he never liked, but he tastes her desire that he like the popcorn in the popcorn and he desires the popcorn. So there they are sniffing desire in roses and tasting desire in popcorn. They must be happy with sex, roses, and popcorn, until the bubble bursts.

Love in Bondage

Let us leave them and look at the implications for autonomy. Though they are happy, they are in bondage. Each is driven by and dependent on the desires of another. As we noted, one can have desires that deprive one of autonomy, but in the case of love, even though one does what one desires and feels the pleasure of it, one is enslaved to the desires of the other because one desires the satisfaction of them. The intensity of the pleasure conceals the bondage. But it reveals itself readily enough. When the loved one desires something that is painful to you, though a romantic sort of masochism might carry the day or night for a while, pain will triumph over desire, and you will know that you do not desire what she desires. She may, of course, desire that someone other than you satisfy her desires, or cease to desire the satisfaction of yours, or cease to love you in the extreme way by rejecting the roses. Desire is rife with conflict, even when another is not involved, and when your desires include the desire for the satisfaction of the desires of another, conflict will manifest itself sooner or later.

So, what do our lovers do? Suppose Rachel finds Matthew's desires, or some of them, unpleasant, and, as a result, no longer desires to satisfy Matthew's desires. The magic is gone. And what is he to do? At first he may continue to desire the satisfaction of her desires, but if she does not desire the satisfaction of his desires, he will quickly enough notice that he is in bondage to her desires. Her desires dominate his desires because he desires the satisfaction of her desires while she does not desire the satisfaction of his. In this situation, he will find her manipulative, though it is his desires that empower her.

He may try to get her to desire the satisfaction of his desires again so that they can return to sniffing desire in roses and tasting desire in popcorn. He may persevere in satisfying her desires to win back her love. But she will see that his actions are not based on his desire to satisfy her desires but on his desire for her to desire to satisfy his desires. This will seem manipulative to her, as it is, and he will not succeed. Finally, he will not desire to satisfy her desires nor she his, each will be astonished that his or her wonderful giving lover has suddenly become a manipulative cad or bitch. The bubble bursts. Pity.

Transcending Extreme Love

Is all this inevitable? Must the magic turn to dust? The danger is great and the way out is hazardous, but let us look at what has gone wrong and, perhaps, we may defeat the pessimists and arrive at a conception of autonomous love. What went wrong? The interaction is driven by first-level desire. First-level desire is rife with conflict, and the conflict must emerge unless one of our lovers is masochistic. I ignore that solution to the problem. The first step is transcendence beyond the first level. We need to ask which desires to satisfy, and, more exactly, how much weight to give to those desires. The simple transcendence from desire to preference takes us in the direction of autonomy. That does not destroy the pleasure of acting on desires, even the desires to satisfy the desires of the other, but it does force the evaluation of them. The bonus of doing so is that when we prefer the satisfaction of desire, it is our preference rather than the desire of the other, even if it is a preference for satisfaction of the desire of the other, that leads us to prefer what we do.

Of course, extreme love for another may enable the other

to manipulate our preferences as well as our desires, and we may be bound at the level of preference. To arrive at autonomy we must prefer to do what we do, including, perhaps, satisfying the desires of a loved one, because we prefer to have that preference to do so. Autonomous love for another should, however, not only express our own autonomy, it should respect the preferences of the other as well. The preferences of the other reflect her transcendence of first-order desire and resolution of first-order conflict. Her autonomous preferences, the preferences that she has because she prefers to have them, represent her ascent to autonomy. My autonomous preference for what she autonomously prefers is or can be a form of love for her that is an expression of my autonomy that respects her expression of her autonomy. We are far from the original magic, but also from the disillusion, of extreme love. Have we found the genuine article of love metamentally embedded in autonomous preference?

Autonomous Love

Let us recall what autonomy requires. A person, S, autonomously prefers A if and only if S prefers A because S prefers to have the preference structure S does with respect to A. Now suppose that S prefers A out of autonomous love for T. How should we analyse the notion of preference out of autonomous love? I propose the following:

(AL) S prefers A out of fully autonomous love for what T prefers if and only if S autonomously prefers A because T autonomously prefers A.[5]

This form of autonomous love contains a prophylactic against the love of bondage and the manipulative consequences of such love. If a lover prefers to do something, prefers to alter his or her plans to accommodate the loved one out of autonomous love, the lover must be autonomous in that preference

---

[5] The connection expressed by 'because' is one of explanation which occurred in the original definition of autonomy.

ence even though he or she prefers what he or she does because the other person autonomously prefers what he or she does. The lover may prefer what he or she does because the loved one prefers what he or she does, but the preference of each is autonomous, and, being so, avoids the love of bondage.

Objections immediately arise, however. For example, someone might, it seems, prefer something out of autonomous love for another when the other does not prefer the thing in question. Deontically directed love, or, as it is called in the current vernacular, 'tough love', arises when I prefer something for another that the other does not prefer; giving up an addiction, for example, or giving up some course of conduct that is harmful to the other, which the other does not prefer but ought to prefer.

My reply to this objection is the one with which I began, namely, that love comes in many forms and flavours. To appreciate the character and the merit of the sort of autonomous love defined above, let us consider the various forms of love and compare them to the ideal offered here.

Forms of Love

I do not deny that other forms of love are worthwhile, including tough love. I am concerned, instead, to look at the full taxonomy of love, for, in fact, I am a great admirer of love, in all the plentiful varieties in which it occurs. Let us consider forms of love that lack some component of fully autonomous love, beginning with the least autonomous and progressing toward the more autonomous, to appreciate the defects as well as the merits of less autonomous forms of love.

Desire and Preference Love

First let us consider love based on desire. We might analyse this as follows:

(LD) S desires A out of love for what T desires if and only if S desires A because T desires A.

This form of love, (LD), the love of desire, might exist between beings who are incapable of transcendence or evaluation of desires. It is a naïve and very charming form of love but is compatible with a complete lack of autonomy. It is the love that Matthew and Rachel have for each other when it first arises, and, when reciprocal, produces the kind of magic enthusiastically enjoyed by lovers at this level. Bondage results from the character of desire which is not within our control. Thus, if love for what another desires is not reciprocated, then since that love is a desire for what the other desires, one is enslaved by one's own desire to the desire of the loved one. One might not mind or notice, but desire being what it is, conflict will arise. When it does, the bondage is noticed and protested against as a form of manipulativeness by the other, and, finally, resented.

Next, consider a form of love which is a preference of the lover for the desires of the loved one. It is as follows:

(PD) *S* prefers *A* out of love for what *T* desires if and only if *S* prefers *A* because *T* desires *A*.

The second form of love, (PD), the preference for what another desires, requires one component of autonomy in the lover, preference involving higher-order evaluation, but allows for a complete lack of autonomy in the loved one. It is characteristic of the love of an adult for a young child. The adult, having reached the age of preference which the child has not, prefers something the child desires just because the child desires it.

In the case of adults, there is, again, a kind of charm in such love, but, assuming the loved one to have the powers of preference, and, indeed, those of autonomy, such love can become a form of condescension and may be resented if the loved one prefers not to have the desire satisfied that the lover prefers to satisfy. If, for example, the loved one is trying to avoid eating chocolate, though he desires to eat some, and the lover prefers to satisfy his desire by supply-

ng a box of exquisite chocolates, the preference of the lover
may be resented because his preference not to satisfy his
desire to eat chocolates is not respected by the lover.

Consider a third form of love based entirely on preference, as follows:

(PL) S prefers A out of love for what T prefers if and only
if S prefers A because T prefers A.

This third form of love, (PL), presupposes preference, a
constituent of autonomy, in both the lover and the loved
one, but it allows for the possibility that the preferences of
either or both are internally compulsive or externally manipulated. Two people who love each other in this way
may be manipulated by the love by a third party, or, for
that matter, by each other and their co-dependence.

This form of love, if reciprocal, is based on the evaluation of desire rather than submission to it, which brings it
closer to autonomous love, but it may fall far short. For it
leaves open the possibility that the lover is not worthy of
his or her own trust concerning what he or she prefers, perhaps because the intensity of need or feeling overpowers
his or her capacity for being trustworthy concerning what
he or she prefers.

One may be less likely to resent a lack of reciprocation in
this kind of love because the preference of the lover is
based on the other's preference, provided, of course, one's
preference for what the loved one prefers is not based on
accepting that she will reciprocate. In this kind of love, lack
of reciprocation may create only disappointment and dis-
couragement rather than resentment and accusation. One
may, with reflection, discover that the preference is compelled and note that one is not autonomous. Compulsive
preference, however backed by justification from one's
evaluation system, is no guarantee that one has progressed
far beyond the dissatisfactions of extreme love. We think of
justified preference as autonomous, but we may be deceived in this. If our preferences are compulsive or manip-

ulated, the bondage of extreme love is reproduced at a
higher level of evaluation, however invisible such bondage
may be and may remain.

We can obtain a more autonomous form of love by
adding that the lover has autonomous preference for the
preferences of the loved one. The definition is as follows:

> (UL) S prefers A out of unilateral autonomous love for
> what T prefers if and only if S autonomously prefers
> A because T prefers A.

This form of love, (UL), requires the autonomy of the lover
but allows for the possibility that the preferences of the
loved one are manipulated. It allows for the case in which
the lover, who is autonomous, controls the preferences of
the loved one and has an autonomous preference for what
the loved one prefers because of having shaped or produced those preferences. The intent of the lover may be
benevolent in forming those preferences in the loved one.
The loved one may be ambivalent or resentful, however, if
the autonomous preferences of the lover for what is preferred by the loved one are perceived as being based on the
lover's satisfaction with having formed those preferences.

All of these four forms of love allow for lack of autonomy on the part of either the lover or the loved one, with
all the potentiality for manipulation of the non-autono-
mous person and resentment resulting from perception of
it. These are, therefore, all forms of love that may be pur-
chased at the cost of the autonomy of one of those involved.
We should not conclude that these forms of love are without value. They all may have value, and the last three, based
on preference, may even be wise.

Whether they are wise will depend, of course, on
whether the loving preference is justified by the evaluation
system of the lover and on whether the justification is undefeated by error. The potential difficulties with these
forms of love are, in fact, objections to the preferences of
lover which must be met, that is, beaten or neutralized. The
potentiality for manipulation in these forms of love and the

possible consequences of such manipulation are competitors for the preference, and the loving preferences are wise only if the competitor can be beaten or neutralized in the particular case.

The most effective response to objections concerning manipulation is that the preferences of the lover and loved one are autonomous, that is, that the love is fully autonomous. Such love was defined as follows:

> (AL) S prefers A out of fully autonomous love for T if and only if S autonomously prefers A because T autonomously prefers A.

However, there are cases in which one can meet competitors to the loving preferences even though they are not based on the autonomous preferences of the loved one.

Perhaps the most familiar form of justification for autonomous love is based on preferences for what the loved one ought to prefer. That is defined as follows:

> (UO) S prefers A out of unilateral autonomous love for what T ought to prefer if and only if S autonomously prefers A because T ought to prefer A.

Unilateral autonomous love for what the loved one ought to prefer, the fifth form of love, (UO) has a more complicated relationship to autonomy and is the sort of love advocates of tough love recommend. It does not require that the lover prefer what the loved one desires or prefers; indeed, the unilateral autonomous lover may prefer the opposite of what the loved one prefers or desires because the loved one ought not to prefer or desire what he or she does. There is no doubt that this is an important form of love and, in some cases, appropriate as well. Nevertheless, there is a dismal history of hostility toward those who love in this way by those who are loved which, even when unjustified, is a cost that should not be ignored and may make such love unwise.

The conflict between unilateral autonomous love for what the other ought to prefer and fully autonomous love for what the other autonomously prefers is one of the most profound conflicts in human relations. This form of unilateral love is one kind of moral paradigm, but it falls short of the paradigm of love. Morality and love may clash, of course, but it is love that concerns me here. Autonomous love seems to me to be the highest form of love, however immoral the lovers might be in what they prefer. Perhaps that is why it is comparatively easy to identify with characters in fiction who love autonomously but live wantonly. We identify with their love as we condemn their wanton preferences. The attempt to reduce morality to love is a philosophical mistake. It is comparable in defect to the attempt to reduce morality to reason. One may love and reason immorally and autonomously.

Autonomous love is, in contrast to the other forms of love, a form of love based on mutual autonomy, as is clear by consideration of our definition of it.

> (AL) *S* prefers *A* out of fully autonomous love for *T* if and only if *S* autonomously prefers *A* because *T* autonomously prefers *A*.

Autonomous love is expressed by the preferences of autonomous love, based on the autonomy of the lovers. It thus avoids the pessimistic claim that love is bondage and manipulation standing in opposition to freedom and autonomy.

Objections and Qualifications: The Contradiction of Autonomous Love

There are, however, objections other than moral ones to autonomous love. One is that the notion of autonomous love is contradictory. Suppose that *S* prefers *A* autonomously—something implied by *S* preferring *A* out of autonomous love for *T*. Then *S* prefers to have the preference structure *S* has with respect to *A* because *S* prefers to have that preference structure, including the preference for *A* itself. So *S* prefers *A* because *S* prefers to prefer *A*. If, at the same time, prefers *A* out of autonomous love for T, then *S* prefers *A* because *T* prefers *A*. Thus, it appears that *S* must prefer *A* because *S* prefers to prefer *A* in order to be autonomous, and also that *S* must prefer *A* because *T* prefers *A* in order to love *T*.

This objection can be met provided we remember 'because' is being used in an explanatory sense, but it is basic and important for an understanding of love which avoids the bondage dilemma implicit in the idea that if I love another then I am a prisoner of the preferences or desires of the other. I can, in fact, prefer what the other prefers because the other prefers what he or she does without becoming a prisoner of the preferences of the other. Everything depends on why and how I prefer what the other prefers. It all depends on whether I prefer what the other prefers primarily because the other prefers what he or she does, which is, in fact, higher-order bondage, or because I primarily prefer what the other prefers because I prefer to prefer what I do and only secondarily prefer to prefer what the other prefers.

Consider the following two statements:

I prefer *A* because *T* prefers *A*.
I prefer *A* because I prefer to prefer *A*.

The objection is that these two are inconsistent, and my reply is that they are not. My preference for what I prefer must explain my preference for what the other prefers and not *vice versa*. I prefer what *T* prefers because I prefer to prefer to have that preference. That is what combines love with autonomy successfully.

Consider the following analogy. I am asked to review a book for a journal that Stew edits, and I decide to do this to assist Stew. Consider the following two statements:

I prefer to read the book because I prefer to review it.
I prefer to read the book because I prefer to assist Stew.

These statements are not inconsistent. I prefer to review the book because I prefer to assist Stew. I prefer what Stew prefers, that I review the book, because I prefer to prefer what Stew prefers. Though my preference appears to be determined by the preference of another, in fact, my preference is determined by my preference for it.

Scope and Knots of Love

The scope of my autonomous love for another can be either broad or narrow. The limiting case of narrow scope is the case in which I autonomously prefer the preference of another for a single and rather limited action. The limiting case of broad scope is where I prefer all the preferences of the other that she has because she prefers to have them. The term 'love' is vague, however, and there is no answer to the general question of how broad the scope of love must be before one really loves another. Relationships that endure will expand and contract the scope of autonomous love to meet the needs and enhance the pleasures of the lovers. As autonomous love contracts, other forms of love may expand and compensate for the deficit of autonomous love.

Love Knots

There are love knots that conflict with autonomous love. Suppose that another prefers that I prefer what she prefers, not because I prefer to prefer what she prefers, but just because she prefers what she does. In that case, she is preferring that I love her non-autonomously. I think that the preference for such love is common, but it cannot be fulfilled by autonomous preference on my part. A preference of another to be loved non-autonomously can be fulfilled but not out of autonomous love. The preference that I prefer what the other prefers, not because I prefer to prefer what she prefers, but just because she prefers it, is a preference for me to love her in bondage. If I comply, then I am enslaved to her preferences in the way that a person is enslaved to the desires of another in the case of extreme love.

Advantages of Autonomous Love

Suppose, however, that I autonomously love another and prefer her preferences because I prefer to prefer them. I may act in the same way as someone who loves in bondage, for as soon as I determine what the loved one prefers I will prefer it as well. Have I thereby lost my autonomy? If not, what is the difference between autonomously loving another in wide scope and loving another in bondage? The difference may not be visible in the actions that occur at a given point in time. But autonomy is not readily visible in action. A person who does what she wants without acting autonomously may do the same thing as a person who acts from autonomous preference. The difference lies in why you prefer what you do, in the influence of higher-order evaluation and metamental certification. You cannot read off internal aetiology from behaviour. If you take metamental ascent and autonomy seriously, you must give up behaviourism.

There are, none the less, some diachronic implications of the distinction between autonomous preferences and other motives that may reveal themselves in behaviour. Desire changes slowly in response to reasoning and evaluation. If I have intense desires concerning another, say, that the other should have some specific desires and beliefs concerning me, to be with me because I am wonderful for her, then those desires will probably not be altered quickly by evaluation and reasoning. For example, reasoning leading me to the conclusion that the other will not come to have the desires and beliefs I desire her to have will probably not extinguish my desire. Desire is often like that. Full of inertia.

I am left desiring that the one I love will love me in the way that I wish even when evaluation and reasoning convince me that what I desire is hopeless. I am left with the misery of an intense desire I am convinced will not be satisfied. The intensity of desire may cause me to try to get her to love me in the way I desire, though I know this is hopeless. The typical masochistic dysfunction of the unrequited love of bondage lies along this path.

Preference and Evaluation

Autonomous love based on autonomous preference avoids the dysfunctional component. This is due to the fact that evaluation is a component of preference. If the evaluation changes, so does the preference. Thus, autonomous love based on preference is not subject to the bondage of extreme love resulting from the unresponsiveness of desire to higher-level evaluation. Of course, we must not convert autonomous love into a libertarian utopia. Having loved another autonomously may itself create desire for the continuation of the love relationship even when it is evaluated as hopeless. I may cease to prefer to satisfy the desires of the other but at the same time continue to desire to satisfy the desires of the other.

Preference not to satisfy the desires of another does not bring about that result immediately, but it has an effect to the extent that action is driven by preference. In any event, there is a difference between preferring something out of autonomous love for another and preferring it out of bondage to the other's desires. The person who prefers out of autonomous love to satisfy the preferences of the loved one prefers to do so because of a preference for having that preference. The preference is, therefore, not manipulated by another and leaves you with autonomy, provided preference is the spring of action.

Autonomous Love and Trust

It is possible to love another and to love the autonomy of another. To love the autonomy of the other is to prefer that the other prefer what they do, including the loving preferences for your preferences, because they prefer to have those preferences. The preference to be loved autonomously is a preference that accepts the autonomy of the other in love. The natural difficulty in loving autonomously arises from the insecurity one feels when the love one receives is autonomous love. One knows that the very preference that the person has for your preferences is the result of the other preferring to have that preference, and this may disappear with the disappearance of the preference of the other. One may feel that one has no control over whether one is loved and suffer the resulting feelings of vulnerability.

Reciprocal autonomous love must be based on trust in the preferences of the other and, for that matter, on trust in one's own preferences. The sequence of self-trust must be extended to the other in autonomous love. I trust myself. I am worthy of my trust in what I prefer and accept. Suppose I love another, and I trust the one I love. The one I love is worthy of my trust in what she prefers, and I accept that she is. I am trustworthy in what I prefer, and she is trustworthy in what she prefers. Moreover, I can be worthy of my trust and the other can be worthy of my trust, even though both I and the other are fallible. One does not have to be perfect to be worthy of trust or to be trustworthy. Autonomous love is a love founded on trust and on acceptance of and preference for the autonomous preferences of the other.

Autonomous love takes us into a keystone loop that includes the other. My preference for the preferences of the other out of autonomous love is based on my evaluation that I am worthy of my own trust in evaluating whether the other is worthy of my trust. I must trust the preferences of the other when I prefer her preferences out of autonomous love for what she prefers. I trust my preferences for her preferences and accept that they are worthy of my trust. I accept that what I prefer is worth preferring and that what she prefers is worth preferring, and assume our mutual autonomy. If I trust her preferences and accept that she is worthy of her trust and mine, I conclude that she is trustworthy for herself and for me when I prefer what she prefers out of autonomous love for her.

If she is trustworthy in what she thus prefers, then she is reasonable in what she prefers. My trust in her preferences and my preference for what she prefers out of fully autonomous love for her will be reasonable, and may be personally justified as well. I will also be wise in my preference if she is worthy of my trust and my justification for my preferences for her preferences is undefeated by errors, including errors concerning her and her trustworthiness. Wise love is difficult, however, because it is so easy to err concerning the trustworthiness of a lover. The wisdom of loving another may be sustained, however, by loving the other in different ways in different domains. When I know the loved one is not worthy of her trust or my trust in some area of her life where her preferences are hurtful to us both, I may prefer something she does not desire out of autonomous love for what she ought to prefer. This form of love for another may be both moral and wise even though it falls short of the ideal of fully autonomous love.

Trust in oneself and the other in fully autonomous love implies that one accepts both are trustworthy in what they prefer and, hence, reasonable in what they prefer, including the preferences of love. Trust and reason combine to offer us the stability of reason instead of control. Autonomy, trust, and reason are the bedfellows of autonomous love and secure it as best as can be against the fickle flux of fortune.

Preference and Passion

Have we taken the passion out of love by insisting on the importance of autonomy in love? One can have a preference for passion. A preference for passion is, of course, not the same thing as passion, nor does it bring it about. Passion, like desire, arises without our bidding and sometimes against our will. We may, however, have a preference for a passionate life, and though that preference will not guarantee passion, it is an ally of it.

There is a practical conflict between passion and preference which may be resolved creatively. Passion is weakened by reflection and driven by impulse. Preference for passion, however, is the positive evaluation of it. The positive evaluation of passion must certify at least a temporary silencing of the voice of higher-order evaluation to allow one to be driven by first-level impulse, for that is the pleasure of passion. Preferring oneself to be driven by passion can be an autonomous preference, none the less.

If I and the person I love autonomously share a preference for passion, we may love autonomously and passionately. If one prefers passion and the other does not, the less passionate lover may find a preference, an autonomous preference, for the preference for passion in the other, or, on the contrary, prefer not to prefer the other's preference for passion. That is a limitation in the scope of autonomous love. Some of one's preferences may not be preferred by the other, but it is important to remember that one may be autonomously loved with wide scope even when not all one's preferences are preferred by the other.

Degrees of Preference and Egalitarian Love

I conclude with a deeper look at preference. Preference comes in degrees and, consequently, preference is not an all-or-nothing attitude. I may give some preference, some weight or degree of preference, to my preferences and to yours. How much preference for the preferences of the other is enough for love? I cannot find any decisive answer to this question, but I think that giving more weight to the preferences of another than to one's own is highly unstable.

If we reciprocate, we shall find that each prefers what the other prefers. When we begin with opposite preferences, though, reciprocation leads to confusion and cycling back and forth between the preferences of the one person and those of the other. I prefer to go to the ballet, my lover prefers to stay home. If each gives greater weight to the preferences of the other, I will switch to preferring to stay home out of autonomous love for her, and she will switch to preferring to go to the ballet out of autonomous love for me. Autonomous love giving greater weight to the preferences of the loved one has preserved the conflict by switching the preferences of the lover and loved one.

Preference for giving greater weight to the preferences of another, even if that preference is itself autonomous, may pose a threat to autonomy. My preference to give more weight to the preferences of another than to my own preference, though autonomous, may lead to a subsequent sacrifice of my autonomy. For, with that autonomous preference as part of my evaluation system, I may sacrifice my preference for my own preferences as a result of giving more weight to the preferences of another than my own. An autonomous preference for giving greater weight to the preferences of the other than to my own can undo the autonomy that generates that very preference.

If, on the other hand, one gives equal weight to the preferences of another and to oneself, that seems to me to represent a kind of love for the other, equal, at any rate, to the love one has for oneself. It has the additional advantage of giving consideration to the content of what one prefers apart from the preferences of the other, which may ground the preferences in content. This form of egalitarian autonomous love will yield many ties among preferences in cases of conflict. It may, however, be better to flip a coin than cycle back and forth, though the latter may have some charm that the former lacks. Egalitarian autonomous lovers will find that indifference between choices often replaces initial conflict between alternatives.

Negotiation in egalitarian love will tend to favour the preferences of the lover with more intense preferences, and that may necessitate the adjustment of the weights of love to keep the less intense lover from being regularly co-opted. Love, it seems to me, requires adjustment of weights to produce negotiation conducive to the happiness of both lovers. Thus, no fixed scheme, even the egalitarian one, seems essential to the love relationship. The lovers must discover how much weight to assign to the preferences of the one they love, just as they must find out how wide the scope of the weights may be. Putting degrees of preference into the configuration of love allows for infinite variation and possibilities in the love relationship and the theory of it.

Relationships of love and autonomous love are but one kind of relationship regarding the preferences of others. All relationships require the evaluation of the preferences of others and negotiation to resolve conflict among them. In the next chapter, we turn to a consideration of negotiation and consensus resulting from evaluating and assigning weight to the preferences of others. The problem of finding the consensual weights to assign to others to resolve conflict is difficult and vexing. We shall find the solution in a mathematical loop within the keystone.

FOR FURTHER READING

On love:

De Sousa, Ronald, *The Rationality of Emotion* (Cambridge, Mass.: MIT Press, 1987).

French, Peter A., Theodore E. Uehling, and Howard K. Wettstein (eds.), *Midwest Studies in Philosophy*, vol. 10 (Minneapolis, Minn.: University of Minnesota Press, 1986).

Lamb, Roger (ed.), *Love Analyzed* (Boulder, Colo.: Westview Press, 1996).

Nagel, Thomas, 'Sexual Perversion', *Journal of Philosophy*, 65 (1969), 5–17.

Nussbaum, Martha, *Love's Knowledge* (New York: Oxford University Press, 1990).

6

Trustworthiness and Consensus

We turn now from the special relationship of love to a more general consideration of the relationships between the self and others, with the purpose of enclosing ourselves and others within the keystone loop of trust and trustworthiness. The question of whether a person is worthy of trust or is trustworthy arises most naturally concerning others. As we trust others and evaluate whether they are worthy of our trust, however, we trust ourselves and accept that we are worthy of our trust in making that judgement. Finally, as a result of considering others worthy of our trust, we modify ourselves and become more worthy of our own trust as a result of trusting them. Consideration of our relations to others, in addition to its intrinsic interest, has special implications for the keystone loop of self-trust, trust of others, and the trustworthiness of ourselves and others for ourselves and others. We shall enclose the trust of others and the trustworthiness of others within the keystone loop.

Extension of Trust to Others

To place the other in the keystone loop of trust and trustworthiness, let us return to the first-person perspective and extend the sequence of self-trust to the trust of others. Let me return to the sequence of self-trust and extend it through evaluation to the other. Here is the sequence.

I trust myself.
I am worthy of my trust.
I am trustworthy for me.
I am trustworthy for me in what I accept and prefer.

I am trustworthy for me in accepting and preferring my trustworthiness.

I am trustworthy for me in my evaluation of my trustworthiness.

I am trustworthy for me in my evaluation of trustworthiness.

So far the sequence of self-trust extends only to me and to my trustworthiness for me, except for the last claim. If I am trustworthy for me, worthy of my own trust, concerning my evaluations of trustworthiness, I may extend the sequence of self-trust to the trust of others, as follows:

I am trustworthy for me in my evaluation of the trustworthiness of others for me.

Others I evaluate as trustworthy for me are trustworthy for me.

I am trustworthy for me in accepting or preferring what others I evaluate as trustworthy for me accept or prefer.

This extension of self-trust to trust of the other reveals the way in which others, and my evaluation of them, become a source of what I accept and prefer. My positive evaluation of their trustworthiness for me may result in a change in what I accept and prefer, and that change can make me more trustworthy for myself and others. I become more worthy of my trust and their trust as a result of my positive evaluation of their worthiness of my trust.[1]

The positive evaluation by others of my trustworthiness may result in a change in what they accept and prefer, and that change can make them more trustworthy for themselves and for me. They become more worthy of their trust

---

[1] Allan Gibbard has a supporting argument for this in *Wise Choices, Apt Feelings* (Cambridge, Mass., and Oxford, 1990), 179–81. It goes like this: I must trust myself. My present views are, in fact, due in large part to the influence of others. So I must confer some legitimacy to past influences. I have no reason for thinking that, while some past influences were all right, no future influences will be. So I must be open to the possible legitimacy of future influences from others. Therefore, I must see at least some other people as trustworthy.

and my trust as a result of their positive evaluation of my worthiness of their trust.

There is a problem with the idea that I can become trustworthy, even for myself, as a result of evaluating the trustworthiness of others, and that they can also become trustworthy for themselves as a result of evaluating the trustworthiness of others, myself included. It is difficult to see how to find in these evaluations of the trustworthiness of each other the appropriate measure of the trustworthiness of each of us, for we are enclosed within the loop of our mutual evaluations of each other.

Laundry Island

The problem is like the problem of laundry island where each person seeks to make a living by doing his neighbours' laundry. Unless each person has wealth to begin with, they will earn nothing as a result of such laundering activity. But even if they each do have some wealth to begin with, the laundering activity cannot increase it, though some may become more wealthy by obtaining money from others. Each of us can contribute her own trustworthiness in the evaluation of others, and, of course, some may become more trustworthy by obtaining her own trustworthiness from those more trustworthy than she. But it appears that the trustworthiness of all cannot be increased by the evaluation of trustworthiness, any more than wealth on the island can be increased by the doing of laundry. The laundry island analogy is misleading, however. The trustworthiness of us all can, in fact, be increased if the process of evaluation enables us to find the appropriate measure of the trustworthiness of each of us through a process of aggregating the individual evaluations of trustworthiness.

Aggregating Trustworthiness

How do we aggregate the evaluations of the trustworthiness of members of a group by members of the group, to find an appropriate measure of the trustworthiness of members of the group for members of the group? The problem of aggregation becomes most obvious when there is conflict within the group, and conflict is, of course, inevitable. There will be conflict concerning what we accept and prefer, concerning what is worth accepting and preferring, and concerning evaluations of trustworthiness of members of the group by members of the group.

These conflicts mirror the conflicts within a person. The conflicts within are, in fact, often internalizations of the conflicts with others and among others. Some aggregation of conflicting evaluations is needed to resolve conflicts concerning what to accept and prefer. Such an aggregation is to be found in the perspective of the first person. Let us return to the sequence of self-trust to find a measure of our trustworthiness and the trustworthiness of others.

Weighted Trust

I consider some more worthy of my trust than others, and evaluate them accordingly. I give greater weight to those more worthy of my trust and less weight to those less worthy of my trust. Thus, the extension of the sequence of self-trust to others continues as follows:

I evaluate myself and others by giving myself and others weight in what we prefer and accept.

I am trustworthy for me in the way I give weight to myself and others.

I am trustworthy for me in changing what I accept and prefer as a consequence of the weights I give to myself and others.

How do I change what I accept and prefer as a consequence of giving weight to others?

Weighted Averaging as Aggregation

I modify what I accept and prefer in terms of the weight I give to others. Here is a simple model of modification by averaging with the weights I give to others. I begin with a unit vote, a vote of one, and I divide the unit between myself and others as my evaluation of our relative trustworthiness for me concerning the matters in question. I will consider others and myself to be more or less worthy of trust. I will also divide the unit of evaluation among myself and others differently for different issues. I might trust what another accepts in some area of science, quantum physics, in which she is more expert than others, and give what she accepts and prefers to accept in this area more weight. In other areas, I might consider her less worthy of trust and give what she accepts and prefers to accept less weight.

Suppose that I have divided my unit vote among myself and others. These are my evaluations of their comparative trustworthiness concerning some issue. What do I do with these evaluations to improve my own trustworthiness in the matter? If my evaluations of their comparative trustworthiness and my own are themselves trustworthy, then I can improve my trustworthiness by incorporating their trustworthiness into my own in terms of my evaluations of it. They, of course, can do the same.

I assign weights, including possibly a weight of zero to someone that I consider not to be trustworthy at all, to the n members of the group. So I have a weight, w_{ij}, which I assign to each member j of the n members of the group that I am evaluating in terms of their comparative trustworthiness for me with respect to their degree of preference p for accepting some belief b. Here I introduce without comment the idea that preference comes in degrees, except to say that I shall return to such preferences later and distinguish them from probabilities. Thus, one person has a stronger preference for accepting the belief than another, with the values falling between 'having no interest in accepting it', represented by 0, and 'preferring acceptance without any doubt at all', represented by 1.

The conflicts between members of the group are represented by differing degrees of preference. If my degree of preference is included among those of the group, and I assign a weight to myself as well as others, then I should modify my degree of preference for the belief in terms of the weights I have assigned by averaging the degrees of preference of all members of the group for accepting the belief b by the weights that I have assigned to them. Assuming that my initial state, before the averaging to resolve the conflict, is state 0 and that the state I arrive at by the averaging is state 1, the formula for averaging is as follows:

$$p^1{}_i(b) = w_{i1}p^0{}_1(b) + w_{i2}p^0{}_2(b) + \ldots + w_{in}p^0{}_n(b).$$

Therefore, my new degree of preference, $p^1{}_i(b)$, is a modification of my degree of preference based on the weights assigned to the members of the group representing my evaluation of their comparative trustworthiness.

Modifying Preference by Averaging

Why should I modify my degree of preference in this way? I should consider my new degree of preference an improvement based on my evaluations. Notice that a refusal to modify my degree of preference at all would be mathematically equivalent to assigning myself a weight of 1 and everyone else a weight of 0 and averaging. Assuming that I assign others positive weight as an evaluation of their comparative trustworthiness, I would be untrustworthy for myself and others in terms of my own evaluations if I refuse to modify my degree of preference in terms of my evaluations.

The reason for averaging rather than modifying my degree of preference in some other way, is that averaging is the modification which aggregates the degrees of preference of all the members evaluated exactly as I have evaluated them. The weighted averaging is an aggregation that exactly expresses the evaluations of trustworthiness I have assigned, and gives no more or less to any degree of preference than my evaluation of, the weight I have assigned to, their trustworthiness. The aggregated degree of preference,

$p^1{}_i(b)$, incorporates and summarizes my evaluations of our individual trustworthiness concerning the degree of preference we have.

This new degree of preference summarizes my evaluations of the trustworthiness of the members with respect to the issue of accepting the proposition in question. It is more worthy of my trust than the preference, $p^0{}_i(b)$, with which I began in the initial state. My preferences become more worthy of my trust as the result of my aggregating the preferences of others in terms of my evaluation of their trustworthiness.

I have increased my trustworthiness by aggregating the preferences of others in terms of my evaluations of their trustworthiness for me. Suppose, to idealize the situation, that they have done the same, that is, they have increased the trustworthiness of their preferences, pertaining to the issue of preference, by aggregating the preferences of others in terms of their evaluations of the degree to which others are worthy of their own trust. Thus, assume that each of the members of the group has arrived at a state 1 aggregated preference. The conflict may have narrowed, but conflict, nevertheless, will most likely remain. I consider the state 1 preferences of all the members of the group and observe the residual conflict. How should I proceed?

Evaluation of Evaluators

If I consider my new preference averaged from the others in terms of the weights I assigned, I notice that my new preference represents the result of my evaluating the trustworthiness of others. Similarly, their new preferences represent the result of their evaluations of the trustworthiness of others. Consequently, I see that their new preferences call for new evaluations. The reason is that I should evaluate their new preferences as summarizing their evaluations of the trustworthiness of others, and, consequently, I now need to evaluate, not their trustworthiness for me about the original issue, but their trustworthiness for me as evaluators of other members of the group.

Here I must consider reassigning weights to others. For example, I might evaluate someone as very trustworthy with respect to his preference for accepting the proposition if it is a proposition about physics and he is a very good physicist; but, at the same time, I might evaluate him as less trustworthy as an evaluator of others' preferences for believing things in physics. That is, I might think that this person is trustworthy for me about physics but not very trustworthy for me as an evaluator of physicists or other people concerned with physics. Conversely, I might think that someone is a trustworthy evaluator of physicists, for example, a leading sociologist who studies physicists, but not trustworthy about physics, because she does not study physics. In short, a new evaluation of trustworthiness is needed, because we are evaluating something new.

Thus, I might use the same formula as the one above modified to move from a state 1 preference to a state 2 preference as follows:

$$p^2{}_i(b) = w_{i1}p^1{}_1(b) + w_{i2}p^1{}_2(b) + \ldots + w_{in}p^1{}_n(b).$$

By the same argument as above, I should consider this new preference, $p^2{}_i(b)$, as an improvement over the previous one because it is, again, a summary of my evaluations of the trustworthiness for me of the trustworthiness of preferences of others. When all the members of the group arrive at a state 2 preference, the argument just given repeats itself. The new preferences of each member now summarize the evaluations of each member of the group about the trustworthiness of others for themselves as evaluators of others. There is now the new task of evaluating the trustworthiness of others as evaluators of the trustworthiness of evaluators.

Converging Aggregation

It is apparent, however limited our capacity to make discriminations, that each aggregation yielding a new preference leaves us with a new task of evaluating the trustworthiness of others for ourselves. At each state, the refusal to modify one's preference is mathematically equivalent to assigning others a weight of zero and averaging. At each new level of aggregation, one will employ new weights until new information about the trustworthiness of others is exhausted and the weights remain constant. The general formula for modifying a preference from a state x to a state $x + 1$ is as follows:

$$p^{x+1}_i(b) = w_{i1}p^x_1(b) + w_{i2}p^x_2(b) + \ldots + w_{in}p^x_n(b),$$

and the argument for aggregation repeats itself as we arrive at each new state.

Constancy

We shall turn to some informal illustration of this process in interpersonal adjustments of preferences to each other, but first let us note some mathematical consequences. It is natural to think that at some stage in the process of aggregation, the weights I assign will remain constant for later stages. I might be able to distinguish between the trustworthiness of someone as a physicist and as an evaluator of those who concern themselves with physics, but I will find it increasingly difficult to distinguish between the trustworthiness of others as evaluators of evaluators and as evaluators of evaluators of evaluators, and so on into the further levels of evaluation of trustworthiness.

Connectedness

So let us suppose that the weights that each person assigns would become constant after some level. Let us suppose as well that either all members of the group assign positive weight to all other members of the group as they become constant, perhaps because one does not bother to re-evaluate the trustworthiness of others once one decides one has no new information that is pertinent, or all are connected to each other by vectors of positive respect. A vector of positive respect connects a person i to a person j just in case there is a series of members of the group, each giving positive weight to the next member in the sequence, where i is the first member and j is the last member of the sequence, and at least one person assigns positive respect to herself.

Thus all members of group would be connected by vectors of positive respect if they could be thought of as forming a large circle in which each person assigned positive weight to themselves and to the person to their left. This shows that the connection might result from each person assigning positive respect to one other person when at least one assigns positive respect to herself. Similarly, if there is one person who respects herself who assigns positive weight to each person, and each person assigns positive weight to that person, this will also connect the whole group.

The reason that connection is important is that if the connection condition and constancy condition are satisfied at some level, and the aggregation process continues indefinitely, then the aggregation process converges. Put more technically, as x in the equation goes to infinity, my new preferences will converge toward the degree of preference of others. We will all be converging by continued averaging toward some consensual degree of preference, $p_c(b)$. That convergence will give us a solution to the original problem of conflict and to the laundry island problem as well.

Consensual Preference

We might have resolved the conflict more directly if we had been able to find a consensual weight for each person j, w_j, to average the original preferences in a single aggregation. We could find a consensual degree of preference, $p_c(b)$, all members of the group could adopt by averaging in terms of the consensual weights as follows:

$$p_c(b) = w_1 p^o{}_1(b) + w_2 p^o{}_2(b) + \ldots + w_n p^o{}_n(b).$$

The problem would be to find the weights that give us the appropriate measure of the trustworthiness of the person for the members of the group including, of course, the person herself. The striking feature of the process of continuing aggregation described above is that it finds the consensual weights by a kind of mathematical magic as the aggregation continues.

Consensual Weights: A Mathematical Loop

The modification of preferences by aggregation of evaluations of trustworthiness results, mathematically considered, from a modification of the weights which converge toward a consensual weight, w_j, for each member of the group used in the formula above. In fact, the weights toward which the process converges, once the conditions of constancy and connectedness are satisfied, may be computed by the following simple formula:

$$w_j = w_1 w_{1j} + w_2 w_{2j} + \ldots + w_j w_{jj} + \ldots w_n w_{nj}.$$

This formula, which is the formula for determining the fixed point vector of weights toward which the aggregation process converges, obviously contains a referential loop of computation. The consensual weight sought, w_j, is the same one that is used in the product, $w_j w_{jj}$, to compute itself, and the same, of course, is true for all such consensual weights. The appropriate measure of trustworthiness of an individual within the group including herself is found in a mathematical loop in the process of aggregation.

The idealized model of aggregation tells us that as each of us aggregates to improve their trustworthiness by using their evaluations of the trustworthiness of themselves and others, a kind of mathematical magic leads each to converge toward a consensual weight of trustworthiness, resulting from consensus within the group, about the trustworthiness of each member of the group for the other members of the group. When you consider the matter for a moment, it is clear that if we converge toward consensus about preferences, we must be converging toward consensus about how trustworthy each member of the group is for the others.

We start with the initial state preferences of each and, contributing our evaluations of the trustworthiness of each other, we converge toward a consensual preference. That can only be the case if we converge toward a consensus about how much weight to give to each member expressing our consensual evaluation of the comparative trustworthiness of each of us for all of us. The consensual evaluation of trustworthiness emerges as a new evaluation of trustworthiness, and contributes new wealth to the process of evaluation on the island of trust.

Objections: Why Connectedness and Constancy?

There are many questions about the result that we must consider. The most pressing, perhaps, is why the connectedness condition should be satisfied by our evaluations of trustworthiness. It does not take much assignment of positive weight to others to produce connectedness. In principle, no more is needed than each person giving positive weight to one other person, provided the pattern of positive weights is right, but even that might seem to be too much. There may be cases in which connection does and should fail because some member of the group does not merit the respect of anyone in the group and does not assign positive respect to anyone either. Connectedness when combined with constancy guarantees convergence toward consensus, however, and that is a reason for seeking to obtain it.

A further question is why, after the second or third aggregation, when all the information people have about the trustworthiness of members as evaluators of evaluators is incorporated, should the aggregation continue? One reason, already given, is that even if one uses or reuses the same information in continuing the aggregation, the trustworthiness one evaluates is a new kind of trustworthiness, however similar it might be to the previously evaluated kind of trustworthiness. At each level a question arises about how much weight to give to a new kind of trustworthiness. Continuing to give the same answer as the one given at the previous level becomes appropriate when there is no reason to change. If you cannot tell the difference from the previously considered form of trustworthiness, the same evaluation seems called for. Another argument for constancy after a certain level, perhaps the simpler, is that constancy combined with connectedness yields convergence revealing the consensual measure of trustworthiness of the members of the group. This consensual measure permits each of us to amalgamate the information contained in the group about the trustworthiness of each of us.

The Sequence from Trust to Consensus

This model is, of course, highly idealized. But it can be understood as an extension of the sequence of self-trust to others that I might articulate for myself in the first person as follows:

I am trustworthy in changing the way I change what I accept and prefer, in the way that others I evaluate as trustworthy change the way they change what they accept or prefer.

I evaluate myself and others by giving myself and others weight in what we prefer and accept.

I am trustworthy in the way I give weight to myself and others.

I am trustworthy in changing what I accept and prefer as a consequence of the weight I give to others and the weight that they give to others.

I change what I accept and prefer in a trustworthy way by averaging the degrees of acceptance and preference of others in terms of the weights I give to them.

Others change what they accept and prefer in a trustworthy way by averaging the degrees of acceptance and preference of others in terms of the weights they give to them.

A consensus of acceptance or preference reached by

weighted averaging is trustworthy for the members of the consensual group, because the process of weighted averaging aggregates the evaluations of trustworthiness of members of the group to find a consensual measure of the trustworthiness of each.

Application: Negotiating Conflict

The articulation of the model leaves us with many questions about its application. The consensual weights in the model might be thought of as representing a measure of trustworthiness of the members of an ideal group of evaluators and aggregators and, perhaps, for an ideal observer of them. But does the model have any application for less ideal observers? I shall argue for the role of a process of aggregation in actual interpersonal relations that approximates to the process of aggregation described above.

A Thousand Dollar Example

Let us consider the simplest case of conflict between persons, a conflict between two persons. The two people may have different levels of regard for each other, from love to hate, but they need to resolve their differences. Consider the case of allocating a sum between two causes, the causes being perhaps political parties, A and B, and the sum being $1,000. One person, Joseph, wishes to give all of it to A and the other, Mary, wants to give all of it to B. Each might, having listened to the other, modify his or her position somewhat; Joseph might agree to give $900 to A and $100 to B, and Mary might reciprocate, agreeing to give $100 to A and $900 to B. This modification is equivalent to each person giving a weight of 0.1 to the other, a weight of 0.9 to himself or herself, and averaging.

The interesting thing about this negotiation is that if Joseph and Mary continue to modify their allocations to the political parties in terms of these weights, they will converge toward a solution, and in this case it will be to give

$500 to each party. The point is that the conflict can get resolved if each participant in the conflict gives the other any positive weight and keeps modifying what he or she will give to A or B by aggregating. You do not have to meet the other half-way to reach agreement, you only need to meet the other some part of the way and keep aggregating.

The example illustrates the mathematical magic by which continuing aggregation finds consensual weights. The convergence resulting from this process of Joseph and Mary is mathematically equivalent to assigning Joseph and Mary each a weight of 0.5 and averaging their original assignments of $1,000 to one party and $0 to the other. The aggregation toward consensus, $500 to A and $500 to B, magically finds the consensual weights, 0.5 for each. These consensual weights might have be used by Joseph and Mary or some third party to compute themselves by using them to average the original weights of 0.1 and 0.9 each person assigned to the other and to themselves. This simple example fully illustrates the abstract mathematics of consensus described above.

The consensus reached need not have been this consensus. Joseph might have given Mary three times as much weight as she gave to him, out of affection, respect for her trustworthiness in the matter, or some combination of the two. So, he might, for example, have given her a weight of 0.3, himself, 0.7, and she might have given him a weight of 0.1, as before, and herself a weight of 0.9. If they persist in assigning these weights and aggregating, they will converge toward giving A $250 and B $750, which is equivalent to giving Joseph a consensual weight of 0.25 and Mary 0.75 and averaging their original assignments of money.

Mediation

Now suppose that Joseph and Mary cannot agree and accept a third party whom they both respect as a mediator. They might give each other zero weight, out of distrust, stubbornness, anger, or whatever you care to imagine, but

they each give the mediator positive weight as the mediator gives positive weight to them. If, in fact, he gives equal
weight to each of them and they to the mediator, aggregating with the mediator will result in the $500 compromise.
If, however, the mediator gives unequal weights to the two
parties, perhaps accepting that they will be better satisfied
with such an outcome, then the distribution to the two parties will be unequal. Of course, the mediator may, in fact, as
a result of discussion lead the parties to give positive
weight to each other as well. Again, with constancy and
continued aggregation, consensus will result through a
process that is mathematically equivalent to one that finds
consensual weights to assign to all members of the negotiation, including, this time, the mediator.

There are two important aspects to conflict resolution
through negotiation. The first is communication and whatever respect for the trustworthiness of the other this engen-
ders. To obtain agreement or reach consensus, however,
one needs to go beyond communication respect to the respect of assigning weights and aggregating. It is aggregation respect that takes us beyond conversation to a
modification of our preferences and, if continued, to some
consensual preference.

The model may, I suggest, be used to explain how people arrive at negotiated settlements concerning allocations
and other matters. Often, unlike the example just considered, there is no money or other quantity being negotiated,
but the process of aggregation has application, none the
less. In such a case, what gets modified is the degree of
preference. If I want to go to a dance programme, and you
want to go to a movie, and we have agreed to spend the
evening together, then we will find that you have a degree
of preference for the movie and for the dance, and so do I.
We need to modify those degrees of preference, first by
conversation and then, critically, by aggregation. How
much weight each of us gives to the preferences of the other
will depend on a myriad of factors concerning our relationship to each other, the character of the dance programme,

the character of the movie, and so forth. The point is that once degrees of preference are acknowledged, giving weight to the preferences of others and continuing to aggregate represent actual processes of negotiation and accommodation.

Both those who study negotiation and those who mediate as therapists attest to the realism of the model, provided that we do not suppose that the negotiators have numbers on their mind as they give weight to others. The point of the mathematical representation is not to suggest that negotiating parties spend their time thinking about what numbers to assign to others. It is, rather, that the processes of modifying degrees of preference and other allocations are equivalent to mathematical aggregation and may be modelled in such terms.

In the case of political negotiation, for example, one notes a long period of conversation and preliminary skirmishing preceding the process of modification to reach consensus. The usefulness of such apparently bizarre discussions about the place of meeting and shape of tables may be to procrastinate about assigning weights and aggregating. Such procrastination appears reasonable enough once one notices that the assignment of positive weight once it becomes constant, will drive the parties to consensus. One can only opt out by assigning the other parties, including mediators, all a weight of zero, in which case they must either reciprocate or accept your preferences if they continue to aggregate. For if you assign them zero, and they assign you positive weight, averaging will converge toward your preference.

To avoid domination and decomposition of the group into non-aggregating subgroups, you have to discuss matters long enough to be confident you are prepared to assign positive weight and aggregate. That will drive the negotiation to consensus when the parties persist in the negotiation. The role of intermediaries in negotiations and their effectiveness, provided they can obtain the positive respect of both parties, is too well known to require comment. This is implied by the model because the intermediaries assigning and receiving positive weight from parties reluctant to assign positive weight to each other can, as the result of aggregation, find the consensual weights in the process.

Opting Out

The gains within this model of passing beyond communication to aggregation and convergence are obvious, but the opportunity to opt out of the process by assigning others a weight of zero at any stage is also of crucial importance. That amounts to placing others in the situation of either accepting your dominance, which will result if they continue to give you positive weight, or reciprocating by assigning you zero weight, which results in the decomposition of the group. There may be circumstances under which it is unreasonable to compromise or in which one needs to protect oneself from domination by others by assigning others a weight of zero. It may be perfectly reasonable to assign others a weight of zero simply to avoid being co-opted or dominated by the strategies of others. An important role of the opportunity to opt out may be to control strategic weighting by the continuing threat of decomposition. The price of consensus is the honest weight of respect given to the preferences of others.

Group Therapy

Let us consider some applications of the model. The applications of the model to the conditions of therapy, particularly therapy involving groups, is salient. A marriage therapist working with a couple may, as one indicated to me, find herself rejected, assigned a zero weight on the model, by one of the partners, when that partner has decided to leave the marriage. One explanation is that the partner in question perceives the counselling process as one in which the therapist is a mediator connecting them to arrive at consensus with each other. The assignment of zero weight is necessary to shift the counselling from mediation to a divorce.

In a broader family situation, a therapist reported to me the oddity of finding that a young child in family therapy may come to dominate. This happens, she noted, usually when a grandparent enters the group. The explanation is that the grandparent, giving greater weight to the preferences of the child and receiving positive weight from the parents, can shift the consensual weight toward the preferences of the child. The grandparent favouring the child in this way can enable the child to dominate This will occur especially quickly if the child refuses to give positive weight to the parents.

Language

There are other applications of the model to situations in which there is conflict to be resolved among individuals. The model may even extend to the use of words and lexical relations between words about which people disagree. Semantic idiolects differ from each other, but there is communal language. Individuals need not always resolve conflicts between idiolect and communal language, but the model explains how they can and sometimes do. It does so in a way that accommodates a division of labour on linguistic matters, noted by Reid and Putnam, as a result of those more expert and trustworthy in a certain subject receiving greater consensual weight.[2] It is the lawyer we consult, not only about the law, but about application of the terms of his art, 'felony', for example, and their relations to other terms within the law, 'misdemeanour', for example. We do not consult him about terms of medicine or physics. This is the result of our evaluations of trustworthiness and

---

[2] Thomas Reid, *Essays on the Intellectual Powers of Man* (Edinburgh, 1785); and Hilary Putnam, *Mind, Language, and Reality* (New York, 1975), 139–52. For a more detailed account the application of the model to language, see Adrienne Lehrer and Keith Lehrer, 'Fields, Networks and Vectors', in F. Palmer (ed.), *Grammar and Meaning* (New York, 1995), 26–47.

the consensual aggregation of them. The semantics of the communal language is the aggregative convergence to consensus, actual and potential, of the semantics of idiolects in a community connected by respect in matters of language.

Ways of Weighting

There are examples in which we assign weights in a way that is based on an evaluation of the trustworthiness of the others concerning what they prefer. There are other cases in which we are concerned to negotiate or arrive at a consensus which is not based on such evaluations but on the simple need to reduce interpersonal conflict and solve a problem. Notice, however, that it suffices for the formation of a preference that is worthy of one's trust that one has assigned weights to others in a way that is worthy of one's own trust. The point about the model, and the great advantage of it, is that it explains how the consensual preference is a trustworthy preference for all of the parties because it is a trustworthy preference for each of the parties based on his or her self-trust and evaluations of trustworthiness. Self-trust and the worthiness of it enclose others within the keystone loop reinforced with the consensual aggregation of trustworthiness. We improve our trustworthiness by evaluating ourselves and others as they do the same. The keystone loop is reinforced by the loop of mathematical aggregation of mutual evaluations converging toward consensus.

Probability and Preference

Another question concerns the application of the model to preferences as opposed to other measures, probabilities, for example, which one might aggregate. Are degrees of preference for accepting something just degrees of probability? Formally, degrees of preference for accepting something will share some of the mathematical features of probabilities; for example, the values of preference for accepting something might be represented by an interval between 1 and 0.

Moreover, the model might be used to aggregate probabilities, and I have explored with Carl Wagner the aggregation of probabilities in some detail.[3] In my work with Wagner, I was concerned with how to obtain the best or most reasonable summary of information contained in a group at a specific time about probabilities or desirabilities. Here, by contrast, I am concerned with a more diachronic or dynamic model. One advantage of my present approach over the earlier one is the emphasis placed on the reasonableness of assigning others a weight of zero at any stage. The benefit is that it limits the benefits of strategic weighting aimed only at having one's own position turn out to be the consensual one. As long as one knows that others can shift to assigning you a weight of zero at any stage and destroy convergence, one has a motive for giving them a weight that will sustain the process in order to reach consensus. Conversely, one has the protection of being in a position to assign others a weight of zero at any stage if they seek a domination strategy.

Here I am concerned with trustworthiness in acceptance and preference and the evaluation of such trustworthiness. Moreover, the degrees of preference measure something different from probabilities. The reason is that my preference for accepting something depends on my evaluation of the worth of accepting it. This, in turn, depends on systematic relations of what I consider accepting, and not just its probabilities. The most obvious case for distinguishing between probabilities and degrees of preference for acceptance arises in the case of scientific theories whose probability may be low, at least based on the incorrectness of past scientific theories, but which may be worth accepting, none the less. It is the systematic relationship of the

---

[3] Keith Lehrer and Carl Wagner, *Rational Consensus in Science and Society* (Dordrecht, 1981). See also articles discussing this book in *Consensus*, a special issue of *Synthese*, 62 (1985), guest ed. Barry Loewer.

theory to other matters that makes them worth accepting for the purposes of understanding and explaining things to which they are systematically connected in the quest for truth.

We may, however, illustrate the role of systematic considerations and the limits of probability without appealing to the complexities of scientific theory. Consider a pair of very simple examples. Suppose there is a contest in which the contestants are numbered 1, 2, 3, 4, 5, and 6, and there are six trials reported so far. The question is how the contestants will do in the next trial. The columns below represent the trials, and the rows represent the order in which they placed with the first row containing those who placed first, and so on.

Consider, then, the following first table:

First Place	2	1	1	1	1	1
Second Place	1	2	3	4	5	6
Third Place	3	4	5	6	2	5
Fourth Place	4	5	6	2	3	4
Fifth Place	5	6	2	3	4	3
Sixth Place	6	3	4	5	6	2

Most people would, I think, believe that contestant number 1 will win the next contest. They would prefer to accept that hypothesis and any conclusions they can deduce from that hypothesis and other things that they accept. The probability that the number 1 contestant will win is 5/6, of course, but that may not be the decisive factor.

Consider the following second table of results of trials:

First Place	1	2	3	4	5	6
Second Place	2	1	2	2	2	2
Third Place	3	3	1	3	3	3
Fourth Place	4	4	4	1	4	4
Fifth Place	5	5	5	5	1	5
Sixth Place	6	6	6	6	6	1

No one will prefer to accept that the number 1 contestant will win on the next trial. But notice that the probability that the number 6 contestant will place sixth is 5/6, and, as a result, one might be tempted to accept that hypothesis. Of course, the same probability holds for the hypothesis that number 5 will place fifth, 4 fourth, 3 third, and 2 second. If, however, we accept those hypotheses about contestants 6, 5, 4, 3, and 2, it follows from them that contestant 1 will come in first, but that is improbable, having only a probability of 1/6. If one were guided by probabilities alone, then, having accepted the hypotheses that contestants 6, 5, 4, 3, and 2 will finish sixth, fifth, fourth, third, and second respectively, one would go on to accept that contestant 1 will not win, for the probability of that is 5/6 too.

What should one prefer to accept and how strongly? There are a number of solutions to these sorts of problems. The first thing to notice is that by increasing the number of contestants we can increase the probability to as high a level as we wish, so the problem is not one that can be solved by saying that the probabilities are not high enough. The second thing to notice is that one might, in the second case, accept the hypotheses about the performance of all the contestants except the first one and, refusing to draw the deductive conclusion, not accept any hypothesis about the number 1 contestant in the second example. The point that I wish to make, however, is that one might have a greater preference for accepting that the number one contestant will win in the next trial in the first example than that the number one contestant in the second example will not win in the next trial, even though the probabilities are the same, namely, 5/6.

Alternatively, when one notices that acceptance of the hypotheses that contestants 6, 5, 4, 3, and 2 will place as numbered in the second example implies that the number 1 contestant will win in the second example, one might have a weaker preference for accepting those hypotheses concerning contestants 6, 5, 4, 3, and 2 in the second case than one has for accepting the hypothesis that the number 1 candidate will win in the first example. The point is that the implications of other considerations, considerations of deductive closure and consistency, may influence the degree of preference one has for accepting hypotheses. The probability of a hypothesis is not the only thing that can influence our evaluations of the worth of accepting something in a way that is worthy of our trust.

A question remains concerning our preference for what we accept once we have disconnected degrees of preference for acceptance from probability. What is the connection between our degree of preference for acceptance and acceptance itself? The simple answer is that if our preference for acceptance of something, of some proposition p, is greater than our preference for non-acceptance, then we shall accept that p. But it is important to notice that our degree of preference for accepting things will depend on what we accept about the worth of the preference. We shall have a higher degree of preference for those things that we accept to have greater merit and a lower degree of preference for those things that we accept to have lesser merit. Degrees of preference loop back to what we accept about the degree of worth of the preference, just as what we accept about the degree of worth of preference loops back to our degree of preference for accepting what we do about the degree of worth.

A Loop in Degrees

There is a loop of mutual support from acceptance of our trustworthiness concerning what we accept and prefer to our preference for our trustworthiness concerning what we accept and prefer. It is maintained and reinforced in a loop from degrees of preference for acceptance, and preference of those things worthy of our trust, to acceptance of the degree of worthiness of our preference for accepting or preferring them. Our degrees of preference and acceptance of the worthiness regarding those degrees is enclosed within the loop of our trustworthiness of our degrees of preference and our acceptance of the worthiness of them.

That loop encloses our evaluations with the evaluations

of others in a measure of our trustworthiness and the trust
worthiness of others. We take the preferences and accep
tances of others within the loop and change our preferences
and acceptances according to our evaluations of their trust
worthiness and ours. Others, of course, do the same. The
result is a mutual aggregation of our evaluations of trust
worthiness. The individual incorporates the evaluations of
the others in the evaluations of the preferences and accep
tance of others and their trustworthiness for the individual
His or her evaluations of the trustworthiness of others for
himself or herself become, in the ideal case of connected
and constant aggregation, the evaluations of others con
cerning the trustworthiness of each and all.

The aggregated individual evaluations of trustworthi
ness become the consensual evaluations of trustworthiness
Hence, the social evaluations, resulting from the aggrega
tion of the individual evaluations, become the consensua
individual evaluations as well. In the actual case, the aggre
gation will be limited, and the social group will often de
compose leaving us with individual differences and
dissent. The ideal aggregation of trustworthiness lies be
fore us as a choice that is a threat to our iconoclasm and a
promise of the improvement of our trustworthiness.

FOR FURTHER READING

On consensus:

Baccarini, Elvio, 'Rational Consensus and Coherence Methods in
    Ethics', *Grazer Philosophische Studien*, 40 (1991), 151–9.
Baigrie, Brian, and J. Hattiangadi, 'On Consensus and Stability in
    Science', *British Journal for the Philosophy of Science*, 43 (1992),
    435–58.
Baird, Davis, 'Lehrer–Wagner Consensual Probabilities do not
    Adequately Summarize the Available Information', *Synthese*,
    62 (1985), 47–62.

Berger, R. L., 'A Necessary and Sufficient Condition for Reaching a Consensus by De Groot's Method', *Journal of the American Statistical Association*, 76 (1981), 415–18.

Braaten, Jane, 'Rational Consensual Procedure: Argumentation or Weighted Averaging', *Synthese*, 71 (1987), 347–53.

Christiano, Thomas, 'Freedom, Consensus, and Equality in Collective Decision Making', *Ethics*, 101 (1990), 151–81.

De Groot, M. H., 'Reaching a Consensus', *Journal of the American Statistical Association*, 69 (1974), 118–12.

Forrest, Peter, 'The Lehrer–Wagner Theory of Consensus and the Zero Weight Problem', *Synthese*, 62 (1985), 75–8.

Gutmann, Amy, and Dennis Thompson, 'Moral Conflict and Political Consensus', *Ethics*, 101 (1990), 64–88.

Lehrer, Adrienne, and Keith Lehrer, 'Fields, Networks and Vectors', in F. Palmer (ed.), *Grammar and Meaning*, (New York: Cambridge University Press, 1995), 26–47.

Lehrer, Keith, 'Coherence, Consensus and Language', *Linguistics and Philosophy*, 7 (1984), 43–56.

Lehrer, Keith, and Carl Wagner, *Rational Consensus in Science and Society* (Dordrecht: Reidel, 1981).

Levi, Isaac, 'Consensus as Shared Agreement and Outcome of Inquiry', *Synthese*, 62 (1985), 3–12.

Loewer, Barry, and Robert Laddaga, 'Destroying the Consensus', *Synthese*, 62 (1985), 79–96.

Nurmi, Hannu, 'Some Properties of the Lehrer–Wagner Method for Reaching Rational Consensus', *Synthese*, 62 (1985), 13–24.

Rescher, Nicholas, *Pluralism: Against the Demand for Consensus* (Oxford: Clarendon Press, 1993).

Schmitt, Frederick, 'Consensus, Respect, and Weighted Averaging', *Synthese*, 62 (1985), 25–46.

Wagner, Carl, 'On the Formal Properties of Weighted Averaging as a Method of Aggregation', *Synthese*, 62 (1985), 97–108.

On social knowledge and justification:

Hardwig, John, 'The Role of Trust in Knowledge', *Journal of Philosophy*, 88 (1991), 693–708.

Kvanvig, Jonathan, 'Is There an "Us" in "Justification"?', *Synthese*, 62 (1985), 63–74.

Lehrer, Keith, 'Personal and Social Knowledge', *Synthese*, 73 (1987), 87–108.

On degrees of belief and acceptance:

Lehrer, Keith, 'Coherence and the Racehorse Paradox', in Peter A
French *et al.* (eds.), *Midwest Studies in Philosophy*, 5 (1980)
183–92.

Skyrms, Brian, 'Higher-Order Degrees of Belief', in D. H. Mellor
(ed.), *Prospects for Pragmatism* (New York: Cambridge
University Press, 1980).

7

Evaluation and Consciousness

We have followed the sequence of self-trust to reason, knowledge, wisdom, and autonomy. We have extended beyond the self to others, to conflict, and consensus. Now it is time to close the consensual loop and find the consensus within. We are conscious of conflict between ourselves and others, which may be resolved by giving their preferences and acceptances a weight reflecting our autonomous evaluation of them. We consider ourselves worthy of our trust as we evaluate the preferences and acceptances of others. Reciprocal positive evaluation and continuing aggregation will resolve conflict and yield consensus. We are also conscious of the conflicts within. Sometimes those conflicts within are the internalization of conflicts between those we respect. Sometimes they have other origins. Once we move from simple preference to degrees of preference, we may resolve the problem of conflict concerning what degree of preference is worthy of trust by aggregation.

Consciousness, Aggregation, and Content

In this chapter, we shall consider the role of consciousness in evaluation and aggregation. We shall consider the knowledge consciousness gives us of our mental states, including acceptance and preference. We shall explain our knowledge of the content of those states. We shall then turn from aggregation in the mind to aggregation in the brain, and close the keystone loop around mind and body, revealing the unity of a materialized mind and a mentalized body.

Consciousness of conflict, of conflicting preferences, begins the process of aggregation. One function of consciousness is to resolve conflict by revealing it to us. This may explain why, as Freud insisted, conflicts that we cannot resolve, perhaps because they are too painful to us, become inaccessible to consciousness. If consciousness functions to resolve conflict, and resolution is impossible, psychic economy would direct consciousness to some more tractable conflict. There are, moreover, always conflicts to provide a focus for consciousness and to demand an application of it. We are conflict-resolvers by nature, and consciousness supplies us with knowledge of the conflicting states. Consciousness is fallible, of course, and when it extends beyond the proper domain of discovering our mental states to providing an explanation of them, it extends itself from a domain in which it is reliable to one in which it is not. In its proper domain of reporting rather than explaining, however, it remains worthy of our trust.

We must, however, explain the reliability of consciousness and not merely postulate it. As we examine the role of consciousness in the keystone loop of our trustworthiness, we shall discover a loop in consciousness itself. An account of consciousness is an essential component in a theory of our metamental ascent beyond belief and desire, to resolve conflict and reach knowledge, wisdom, and autonomy. We can imagine creatures without consciousness capable of higher-order processing—computers, for example. Our metamental ascent is effected by consciousness, however. Consequently, to understand ourselves, our knowledge, our wisdom, our autonomy, we must understand our consciousness and the knowledge it reveals to us.

Aggregating Internal Conflict

We shall turn to an examination of consciousness and its credentials after first considering the method of aggregation for resolving conflict within. I assume that I am trustworthy in evaluating the acceptances and preferences of others when they are in conflict, and, equally, I accept my

trustworthiness in evaluating my own conflicting preferences and acceptances. The resolution of conflict within by
the application of the method of aggregation is formally
identical to the method of aggregation applied to others.
All of us have multiple perspectives, all of us are amalga-
mations of those we respect and care about, of their beliefs
and desires, and that leaves us with the problem of resolving the conflicts arising from our internal and internalized
persons and perspectives.

The problem of resolving internal conflicts can produce
the same multiplicity of evaluations and assignment of
weights as social conflicts. I can evaluate the preferences of
each perspective from each perspective. As I try to resolve
the conflicts between internalized friends, teachers, parents, colleagues, I can take each perspective and evaluate
the others. Were that not the case, conflict would dissolve
easily in a single assignment of weights to diverse preferences and the averaging of them. But, just as different people can average in terms of the weights that they assign
without reaching consensus in a single averaging, as we
noted in the two-person $1,000 example in the last chapter,
so an individual can average from different perspectives, as
though he or she were a group of individuals with differing preferences and evaluations of the preferences of each
other.

I have perspectives 1, 2, 3, and so on with preferences
corresponding to each of them. As I set out to resolve the
conflict, I move from an initial state 0 to the next state 1
from a given perspective i by the same formula as in the
multipersonal case:

$$p^1_i(b) = w_{i1}p^0_1(b) + w_{i2}p^0_2(b) + \ldots + w_{in}p^0_n(b).$$

In my quest to resolve a conflict between the perspectives, I
may continue to aggregate from each perspective moving
from a state x to a state $x + 1$ by the following formula:

$$p^{x+1}_i(b) = w_{i1}p^x_1(b) + w_{i2}p^x_2(b) + \ldots + w_{in}p^x_n(b).$$

As I continue, as x goes toward infinity, I converge toward an internal consensus or integration.

This process of continued aggregation is mathematically equivalent to an attempt to find a set of consensual or integrative weights to average the original conflicting preferences by the following formula:

$$p_c(b) = w_1 p^o_1(b) + w_2 p^o_2(b) + \ldots + w_n p^o_n(b).$$

Finally, this set of consensual weights is one that might be computed directly by the formula that contains a loop, using the weight to compute itself as follows:

$$w_j = w_1 w_{1j} + w_2 w_{2j} + \ldots + w_j w_{jj} + \ldots w_n w_{nj}.$$

This picture of internal aggregation reveals how my trustworthiness results from the aggregated trustworthiness of the perspectives within. My trustworthiness is a product of the evaluations of each of my perspectives from each of my perspectives and my autonomous aggregation of them. The aggregation is a mathematical representation of my process of modification. It does not require my consideration of numbers and quantities any more than the visual perception of depth requires a consideration by the eye of numbers and quantities that occur in a mathematical representation of the aggregation of factors involved in the perceptual process. The importance of the mathematical representation is that it reveals that I can resolve conflict in a trustworthy way by finding integrative weights to give to conflicting preferences, including preferences about what to accept, from various perspectives, given an autonomous preference for integration.

The most important feature of the mathematical representation, of considering the process of conflict resolution as a process of aggregation, is that it explains how autonomous commitment to a process of conflict resolution, which may be mathematically represented as a process of aggregation to convergence, can resolve conflict from within the perspectives that generate the conflict. There is no need to suppose that there is some super-perspective, some homunculus, that looks at all the other perspectives and decides between them. Conflict resolution feels like shifting and changing perspective in the process of resolution. It is a continuous mental process, an unceasing train of thought. I cannot step outside myself to resolve the conflict, but must resolve the conflict from within the conditions and perspectives that generate it. That is what aggregation does. That will prove important when we turn to consider the relation of mind and body, for as Dennett has insisted, there is no such homunculus in the brain.[1]

Aggregation and Autonomy

Why should the aggregation be autonomous? We have already considered the answer, in part, when we considered the role of autonomy in evaluation. I have no reason to accept that my evaluations, and, consequently, what I accept and prefer, are trustworthy, unless I am their author. For if I am not the author of evaluations, why should I trust them? What is the use of such evaluations to me? If I am not their author, I have no reason to trust them, though another may. It may be objected that my evaluations may be correct, even though I am not their author, and that is a reason for me to accept them. The answer is that such reasons are not my reasons if I am not their author. Ultimately, I must autonomously evaluate whether something is a reason for me to accept or prefer something. Autonomous evaluation is what makes a reason my reason by making me its author.

Of course, I may believe that I am trustworthy, but that will not raise me to the level of acceptance, reason, or justification. That depends on my being the author of my preferences, on my autonomy with respect to them. I cannot, however, step outside my evaluations to evaluate them. My evaluation of my evaluations, like the evaluation of my beliefs and desires, must take place within me; and for them to make me trustworthy, for them to make me worthy

---

[1] Daniel Dennett, *Consciousness Explained* (Boston, Mass., 1991).

of my trust, they must be mine. I must be their autonomous author.

One way of illustrating the importance of my autonomous preference for the aggregation is to consider the cases in which I prefer not to aggregate. In the social context, I may prefer not to aggregate. I may assign others a weight of zero because I consider others to be untrustworthy in their evaluations or because I think that my preferences will be co-opted by others in the process of aggregation. I then express my autonomy in a preference not to assign others any positive aggregation weight. Similarly, in the case of personal rather than social conflict, I may prefer not to aggregate. I might, for example, feel that a perspective is too important to be modified, integrated, or compromised by aggregation. I may prefer the conflict within, as I sometimes prefer the conflict with others, however divided that might leave me or us.

The decomposition of a social group when aggregation fails and conflict remains may be a better alternative than aggregation, and the decomposition of the self may be a better alternative than aggregation as well. Radical change, both personal and social, may be facilitated by decomposition of the self or the society. It can be productive of a new society or a new self. The price, in both cases, is the destruction of an entity, a social group, a social self, but the outcome may be the creation of a new group or a new self. The divided self, like the divided society, contains both the danger of dysfunction and the hope of transcendence. It is, consequently, important to our integrity, to our trustworthiness, that the preference to aggregate or not to aggregate be autonomous. It is the preference by which we decide whether to aggregate the perspectives within as we do in the normal course of life, or pursue the danger and hope of more radical change. The trustworthiness of the self is articulated in the way in which conflict is met, whether in the resolution of aggregation or the decomposition of the self. It is my autonomous preference that maintains my trustworthiness whatever path I choose.

Knowledge of Lucid Content

What, then, is the role of consciousness in the autonomous preference? It is, of course, to tell us of the conflict, to inform us of the preferences and desires, acceptances and beliefs, within. Consciousness is our epistemic means for ascending to a level at which we can exercise autonomy. Without knowledge of the conflict, there can be no autonomous resolution of it. It is consciousness that provides the knowledge of conflict, as it provides knowledge of our mental life. We need, however, to note the opposition to the idea that consciousness can give us knowledge of our inner life.

Some philosophers and cognitive scientists have had their doubts about whether consciousness can supply us with knowledge of our own mental states.[2] These doubts have focused on the capacity of consciousness to give us knowledge of the contents or objects of beliefs and desires. There are, however, some mental states, our acceptances and preferences, whose content is often epistemically lucid. We know without effort or reflection what we accept and prefer at the time at which the things accepted or preferred are the objects of our present thoughts concerned with the positive evaluation of them. This sort of knowledge of the content of our own mental states, I call *lucid content*. Some of our mental states may be epistemologically opaque in the sense that we are ignorant of their existence until we engage in scientific investigation.

Other mental states are, however, epistemologically transparent in the sense that we know of their existence prior to any such investigation. The latter include our present thoughts and the content or intentional objects of those thoughts.

What I wish to argue is that lucid content should be taken seriously as part of the database for philosophy and cognitive science. It should be treated as evidence on a par

[2] Cf. Tyler Burge, 'Individualism and Self-Knowledge', *Journal of Philosophy*, 85 (1988), 649–63.

with external perception.[3] There have been some reasons that have led philosophers and others to doubt that such knowledge should be taken seriously. It has been noted that judgements about our mental states may be in error, that is, that such judgements are fallible.[4] Fallibility is, however, a ubiquitous epistemic condition and, therefore, not a good reason for rejecting any knowledge claim. We can be both fallible and trustworthy, and trustworthiness must suffice for knowledge.

Scepticism about Consciousness

Consider an example. If I turn my thoughts to what I see, I think that I see a monitor. That is the lucid content of this thought, that I see a monitor. I accept that the content of my thought is just that, that I see a monitor, because I am conscious of that thought. How I am so, we shall soon consider, but now let us focus on my acceptance that the content of my thought, what I am thinking, is that I see a monitor. Is this acceptance and knowledge appropriate to the database of science or is it just an error of folk psychology, like demons in wooded caves and spirits in running brooks? Is the acceptance of the lucid content of a thought an error? That is a sceptical doubt. How should the doubt run?

It might run with the swiftness of the eliminative materialist. The only thing that is intersubjectively observable is matter. It is only matter, in this case, brain matter of neural assemblies that we posit in a scientific theory of the mind. When a person accepts that he is thinking that he sees a monitor, what is really going on is that the monitor activates the senses resulting in neural activation in the neural assemblies of the brain. Putting the point crudely, what the person accepts as thinking that he sees a monitor is an

[3] Cf. Lynne Rudder Baker, *Saving Belief* (Princeton, N.J., 1987).
[4] Cf. Stephen Stich, *From Folk Psychology to Cognitive Science* (Cambridge, Mass., 1983); and Paul Churchland, 'Eliminative Materialism and Propositional Attitudes', *Journal of Philosophy*, 78 (1981), 67–90.

error. All that is going on is vector multiplication in the brain.[5]

Schematically put, the issue runs as follows in a dialogue between myself, who claims what I just have, and an eliminative materialist cast as a sceptic.

> Claimant: I accept that I am thinking that I see a monitor.
> Sceptic: You are not thinking that you see a monitor, for all that is going on is vector multiplication in your brain.

Can I meet this sceptical objection? The reply seems pretty straightforward.

> Claimant: I am conscious of my thinking that I see a monitor, and consciousness of the content of my thoughts is a trustworthy source of information.

This answer is an appeal to my evaluation system.

Now we might imagine the sceptic replying as sceptics are wont to do.

> Sceptic: Consciousness, whatever that is, leads us to make errors and, therefore, is not a trustworthy source of information.

The reply of the claimant is simplicity itself.

> Claimant: All of our sources of information sometimes lead us to make errors, but that does not show them to be untrustworthy. Moreover, I accept that consciousness is a trustworthy, though fallible, source of information, and I am trustworthy in what I accept.

The last reply of the claimant is intended, of course, to forestall further objections. Recall what we said about personal justification in the second chapter, namely, that it results from the capacity to defend what one accepts against

---

[5] Paul Churchland, 'Eliminative Materialism and the Propositional Attitudes'; Paul Churchland, 'Reduction, Qualia, and the Direct Introspection of Brain States', *Journal of Philosophy*, 82 (1985), 8–28.

objections on the basis of the evaluation system of the subject. What the claimant says suffices to personally justify him in accepting what he does about the lucid content of his thought in terms of his evaluation system, which, in this case, is my evaluation system. If, moreover, the claimant's claims are correct, then the personal justification, assuming there are no other objections that cannot be met, will convert into knowledge. Simply put, the sceptical objection is met by being beaten. It is more reasonable for the claimant to accept what he does than to accept what the sceptic alleges.

If this reply seems doubtful to you because you are inclined to distrust consciousness as a source of information, you may be unable to assume the position of the claimant. For example, you might have considered the fact that people often err in the explanations they give for doing what they do and conclude, fallaciously as it happens, that since consciousness does not give us knowledge of the causes of our actions, it does not give us knowledge of the existence of our present thoughts either. Or you might be impressed by some other failure of consciousness to supply you with some other truth about your mental states. How might we argue that you should relinquish your scepticism?

Perception and Consciousness

Suppose that you are not inclined to be a sceptic about perception, and, though you have doubts about whether consciousness yields knowledge of lucid content, you do not have such doubts about whether perception yields knowledge of the monitor. You will then find that you are involved in an exactly analogous dialogue with a sceptic who maintains that you do not perceive a monitor at all, that there is only vector multiplication in the brain. The dialogue will proceed as follows.

  Claimant: I accept that I see a monitor.
  Sceptic: You are not seeing a monitor, for all that is going on is vector multiplication in your brain.

Claimant: I perceive a monitor, and perception of objects is a trustworthy source of information.

Sceptic: Perception, whatever that is, leads us to make errors and, therefore, is not a trustworthy source of information.

Claimant: All of our sources of information sometimes lead us to err, but that does not show them to be untrustworthy. Moreover, I accept that perception is a trustworthy, though fallible, source of information, and I am trustworthy in what I thus accept.

In short, the defence of perception of external objects against scepticism is exactly parallel to the defence of consciousness of lucid content against scepticism. Thus, if perception is worthy of scientific trust, so is consciousness. If you accept that you perceive the external world, you should accept that you are conscious of the internal world, though both perception and consciousness are fallible. Moral: You do not have to be perfect to be trustworthy, and being trustworthy suffices for justification.

It should be noticed that the objection of a more modest sceptic cannot be beaten, but may be neutralized to attain personal justification based on the evaluation system of the subject. Suppose our materialistic sceptic puts forth a more modest hypothesis, one compatible with token–token identity theory, for example, the hypothesis that what is going on in the brain when I think is neural activation. So the dialogue goes like this:

Claimant: I accept that I am thinking that I see a monitor.

Sceptic: What is going on in the brain is neural activation.

This sceptical hypothesis cannot be beaten, for it is something that it is highly reasonable to accept, but it may be neutralized. For the claimant may reply as follows:

Claimant: I accept both that I am thinking that I see a monitor and that what is going on is neural activation. It is just as reasonable for me to accept both as to

accept one, and the combination does not compete
with my original claim.

The claimant may have more than one explanation for
why the acceptance of both claims is as reasonable as the
acceptance of one, but the most standard explanation
would be in terms of the token–token identity of the event
of thought and the event of neural activation. This explanation would have the consequence, however, that the event
of neural activation has content, indeed, the content that I
see a monitor, because the thought event has that content.
We would then be left with the problem of attributing intentionality to events of neural activation, and explaining
how we can have knowledge of the existence of events that
are identical to neural events of which a person may be
completely ignorant, when she has knowledge of the lucid
content of what she is thinking, accepting, or preferring.

Intentionality and Materialism

Some philosophers have considered that attribution of intentionality, of lucid content, to neural activation is implau-
sible unless the attribution can be reduced to the attribution
of known properties of matter.[6] If the reduction is impossible, they would conclude that the attribution of intentionality must be erroneous. But this conclusion is badly drawn,
and we should not allow ourselves to be drawn to it. Our
knowledge of the lucid contents of our thoughts, of what
they are about, of their intentional objects, however one
cares to put it, is a known fact for science to explain. It is
not the business of philosophy or science to deny known
facts to simplify our theories or fit our reductionistic
methodologies.

A philosopher or scientist who knows that her thoughts
have lucid content will attribute lucid content to the body
and, most plausibly, to neural activation in the brain. If, as

[6] Cf. Paul Churchland, 'Reduction, Qualia, and the Direct Introspection of Brain States'.

some philosophers have held, the attribution of intentionality to the brain mentalizes the body, then the mentalization of the body is a necessary condition of accounting for our knowledge of it. We know that our thoughts have lucid content. However, we shall find that the mentalized body, like the materialized mind, are both features of a mathematical reality to which our enquiry will lead us in the last chapter. There is philosophy beyond mentalism and materialism.

Consciousness of Lucid Content

The problem that now confronts us is to account for our knowledge of lucid content. Standard accounts of wide and narrow content shroud our knowledge of the content of our thoughts in mystery.[7] Let us begin with the assumption that thought is mental tokening, though, in fact, other accounts of thought will do quite as well. I begin with this assumption because it is heuristically useful for the purposes of explaining how consciousness can give us knowledge of content. I shall argue later that we may dispense with the assumption that thought is mental tokening for the purpose of explaining our knowledge of lucid content from consciousness. Accounts of wide and narrow content fail to explain such knowledge even given the assumption that thought is mental tokening.[8]

Standard accounts of wide content explicate wide content in terms of causal ætiology or covariation with the tokening.[9] These accounts are difficult to render plausible because of the multiplicity of causes and reasons we have for tokening a sentence, only one of which is an accurate

[7] Cf. Jerry Fodor, *Psychosemantics* (Cambridge, Mass., 1987), and 'Cognitive Science and the Twin-Earth Problem', *Notre Dame Journal of Formal Logic*, 23 (1982), 98–118.

[8] Alvin I. Goldman, 'The Psychology of Folk Psychology', *Behavioral and Brain Sciences*, 16 (1993), 15–28, and 'Consciousness, Folk Psychology, and Cognitive Science', *Consciousness and Cognition*, 2 (1993), 364–82.

[9] Jerry Fodor, *The Language of Thought* (New York, 1975), and *Psychosemantics*.

description. The problem that arises from equating lucid content with wide content, however, does not depend on such details of causal ætiology. The problem is the ease and immediacy with which we know the contents of some of our thoughts. Our knowledge of their lucid contents is mysterious on the assumption that lucid content is wide content. We have no way of knowing ætiology or covariation with armchair ease and immediacy.[10]

Narrow content might be thought to fare better, but narrow content construed as the functional role of a token in a complex network of nomological relations does not explain lucid content either, for we have no way of knowing the functional role with ease and immediacy either. Some internal state that in some way accompanies narrow content or wide content might, of course, be known immediately, but knowledge that the internal state accompanied narrow content would be necessary for our knowledge of lucid content to be knowledge of narrow content. This knowledge would, again, lack the ease and immediacy of our knowledge of lucid content. Moreover, we would still need an account of how we know of the accompanying internal state. The conclusion is not that such functional theories are false, but rather that the defence of them requires a supplemental account of our knowledge of lucid content.

The preceding remarks concerning wide and narrow content should not be taken as criticisms of those views as explanations of the nature of the content of our thoughts. A correct theory about the nature of some entity may leave us with a mystery about how we know of the existence of such entities. My argument is not that such theories are defective because they fail to supply us with a theory of how we know the contents of our thoughts. It is that such accounts must be supplemented with a theory of how we know. I shall now proceed to offer the supplement.

[10] For an argument to the contrary, see John Heil, 'Privileged Access', *Mind*, 97 (1988). An extended version of the argument can be found in John Heil, *The Nature of True Minds* (New York, 1992).

Consciousness and the Metamental Loop

Suppose, then, that a thought is a mental tokening, that is, a tokening of some mental sentence. How do we know the lucid content of the sentence tokened? The answer is that consciousness produces a nexus of metamental ascent and descent, realized as quotation and disquotation, that, combined with our understanding of the sentence, yields our knowledge of lucid content. Consciousness creates a kind of metamental loop from quotation of the token back on the token itself as an exemplar of something having a certain kind of function or role.

Let me explain by appeal to another loop. Consider the sentence

(S) This sentence refers to itself.

How do we know that this is true? The sentence refers to itself and tells us that it is true. Understanding the sentence suffices for knowing that the sentence is true because, in referring to itself, it becomes an exemplar of a class of tokenings that refer to themselves and to which it belongs.

Now consider the sentence of thought,

(M) I see a monitor,

the tokening of which is my thought. How does consciousness give us knowledge of the content of this thought involving the token (M)? Consciousness gives us metamental ascent by quoting the sentence, and metamental descent by disquoting the sentence, to yield

(LC) 'I see a monitor' has the content that I see a monitor.

The yield is, of course, not very informative, but, if I understand (LC), then it tells me the content of my thought. The trick of consciousness is to effect a loop from the token back onto itself as a token representing an understood class of tokens. The final four words in (LC) reuse the token to refer to a class of tokens of which it is a member, and identify the class by exhibiting itself as a member of the class.[11]

It is very important to an understanding of the role of consciousness in our knowledge of lucid content not to confuse the original tokening of the sentence with the quotation of the token. Even the sentences

(M) I see a monitor

and

(MT) The sentence 'I see a monitor' is true

do not have the same content or meaning. Sentence (M) does not entail that there are any sentences, it only says that I see a monitor, while sentence (MT) entails the existence of the sentence. Yielding (LC), consciousness adds to our understanding by means of the metamental loop of the token onto itself.

Knowledge of Consciousness

It is now simple enough to understand how consciousness gives us knowledge of the lucid contents of our own thoughts. Consciousness reveals what a sentence is about by the loop of metamental ascent and descent using the sentence itself to reveal what the sentence is about. Moreover, in revealing what the sentence is about, it can reveal itself as the revealer of this fact. Consciousness can reveal itself in the same way that light does. Light in revealing the illuminated object can reveal itself at the same time.[12] Thus our knowledge of the lucid content of our thoughts can, at the same time, give us knowledge of our consciousness of that content. Consciousness can become consciousness of itself at the same time as it is consciousness of content. Not all conscious states loop back upon themselves in an operation of metamental ascent and

[11] Wilfrid Sellars, *Science, Perception and Reality* (New York, 1963).
[12] Thomas Reid, *Essays on the Active Powers of Man* (Edinburgh, 1785), Essay 6, ch. 5, Principle 7.

descent. A young child, for example, may lack the capacity for the operation and, as a result, both think and be conscious without the content of either becoming lucid.[13] Thought and consciousness of the thought may, in an adult, become lucidly known in the metamental loop of exemplarization.

We may remove the mystery of supposing that some token can be made into an exemplar or, in a sense, a symbol of a class of things to which it itself belongs, by considering some other examples. A token of a song can stand for a class of tokens of a given kind or type.[14] A token of a song may be sung as an exemplar of the class of tokens of a song. So, for example, if I tell you that my favourite pop rock song is the *Shoop Shoop Song*, and you want to know what the song is, I might sing it for you, or, much better, get Cher to sing it for you. The token produced serves as an exemplar of the tokens of the song. If you are inclined to think of the song as the class of token singings, then the token sung will stand for the class at the same time as it is a member of the class. If you are inclined to think of the song more platonistically as a song of certain kind, then the token sung will stand for a kind which has the class of tokens as instances. There is, however, a loop of reference from the token to a class of tokens of which it is a member.

Knowledge of Sensations and Exemplarization

The nexus of consciousness supplying a loop from a token back on itself as an exemplar of a kind of token to give us knowledge of lucid content has more general implications. The metamental loop of consciousness can convert mental states into symbols in a way that accounts for our immediate knowledge of many of our mental states, not just our intentional states. Consider our knowledge of sensations which are alleged not to be intentional. The metamental

[13] Cf. Alison Gopnik, 'How we Know our Minds: The Illusion of First-Person Knowledge of Intentionality', *Behavioral and Brain Sciences*, 16 (1993), 1–14.
[14] Cf. Nelson Goodman, *Languages of Art* (Indianapolis, Ind., 1968).

loop of consciousness can yield knowledge of those states, of a pain, for example, by making a symbol out of the pain. We can take the pain to stand for other pains and thus use it to represent pains. Our knowledge that we are in pain can result from the metamental loop of consciousness using the pain as an exemplar or symbol of pains. The process I call *exemplarization*.

This process of exemplarization explains the traditional doctrine of our incorrigible knowledge of our mental states. Using the state as an exemplar to stand for a class of states, we would seem invulnerable to error in believing that the state belongs to a class of which it is an exemplar. Unfortunately, consciousness, like perception and other faculties, can misfunction in the production of the nexus and lead us into error. We need the assumption, noted above, that consciousness is a trustworthy source of information, which introduces the coherence that may convert into knowledge. Moreover, a particular pain, though it may represent pains generally, is a poor symbol for the purposes of memory and communication. Consequently, other symbols are needed, like the word 'pain', which are subject to all the hazards of erroneous application. To store and communicate our knowledge of our mental states we must map them onto more conventional symbols than the metamental loop of consciousness can provide. It may, however, provide us with some relief from the arrows of scepticism to recognize that the metamental loop of consciousness can provide us with knowledge of the lucid content of thoughts and of the existence of other mental states, though, it goes without saying, only those of which we are conscious.

Lucid Content without Mental Sentences

Consideration of the way in which a metamental loop can provide us with representation and knowledge of mental states will allow us to dispense with the assumption that all our knowledge of the lucid contents of our thoughts depends on mental sentence tokens. The thesis of one version of the computational theory of mind ascribes mental tokens in the language of thought to us as explanatory entities.[15] It is possible, however, that the advantages of such a theory might be obtained without the postulation of such entities, as I have argued elsewhere following Thomas Reid, provided that operations of thought have sufficient logical and semantic complexity.[16]

Of course, there are sentences that occur in thought, the sentences of conventional languages, English, Spanish, Esperanto, and so forth. We use such sentences to articulate our thoughts to ourselves or others. The metamental loop operates on these to give us knowledge of them. The postulation of an innate language of thought used to interpret these sentences and other expressions of conventional languages goes beyond the data to theory and the postulation of theoretical entities. That is not a criticism of such a strategy, but I prefer not to tie the account I am presenting to the postulated tokens of a theory of the innate language of thought.[17] We have an innate capacity to convert our mental states into symbols by exemplarization and construct a system of them, but that system is constructed from the symbol maker within us and is not an innate language of thought common to us all. We diverge in the symbol systems we make in thought and aggregate to resolve our differences in public languages as the need arises.

Lucid Content without Mental Tokens

Fortunately, it is not difficult to extend the account of how a metamental loop gives us knowledge and representation of mental operations to yield an account of lucid content, without postulating the existence of mental tokens in a innate language of thought. There can be thought processes having lucid content without any mental token having that content. For example, suppose that there is some operation,

[15] Jerry Fodor, *The Language of Thought.*
[16] Keith Lehrer, *Thomas Reid* (New York, 1989), ch. 15.
[17] Cf. Jerry Fodor, *The Language of Thought.*

O, of the mind that has the content that I am thinking that I am in pain. That operation, *O*, can be used to represent itself and other operations of the same kind in the way the individual pain or feeling can be used to represent itself and other things of the same kind. This self-representation is exemplaric representation. The metamental loop can start from any operation of the mind, a sensation of pain or colour, for example, and, by means of the loop of metamental ascent and descent, yield an exemplaric representation of the operation by exemplarization. Looping can, in principle, convert any mental operation of which we are conscious into an exemplaric representation and, by so doing, yield immediate knowledge of the mental state.

Consciousness and Materialism: Jackson's Argument

Jackson has appealed to our knowledge of conscious states to formulate an argument against materialism.[18] Suppose that a person has all the knowledge it is possible to have about the material states of the world and of a person. Now imagine that a person has such complete knowledge of the material states of people but has never been conscious of certain qualities, for example, of colour. Jackson asks us to suppose that a person, Mary, who has complete knowledge of the material states of people and of physics generally, has lived her life in a monochromatic room. Though she has complete knowledge of the material states of people who are conscious of colour, red say, she has not herself been conscious of any colours. There is a kind of subjective knowledge that she lacks and which she could acquire by leaving the room and becoming conscious of colours. She would then know what red is like when she did not know this previously in her monochromatic life.

The argument offered by Jackson is intended as an argument against materialism, as an argument against the view that materialism could be a complete account of the world

---

[18] Frank Jackson, 'Epiphenomenal Qualities', *Philosophical Quarterly*, 32 (1982), 127–36.

and our knowledge of it. But, as Ferrier noted long before Jackson and even Nagel, it is an argument against objectivism.[19] Let objective knowledge be any knowledge of things that is objective in the sense that, in principle, it could be represented objectively so that anyone could acquire the knowledge from the objective representation of it. Now suppose that we have such a representation of the consciousness of something. A person who only had knowledge of such consciousness from the objective representation of it would inevitably lack some knowledge concerning the consciousness of it, namely, knowledge of what it is like to be conscious of the thing in question. The perplexity is that subjective knowledge is knowledge of fact but is subjective and transcends all scientific or objective knowledge.

This argument has been much discussed, and the solution often proposed is based on the opacity of knowledge contexts. A person can know that p and fail to know that q when the assertion that p and that q represent the same fact but in different ways. Thus, a person can know that Mark Twain is an author and fail to know that Samuel Clemens is an author when the assertion that Mark Twain is an author and the assertion that Samuel Clemens is an author represent the same fact but in different ways. The reason that the fact is the same is, of course, because Mark Twain is Samuel Clemens, they are the same person, and, consequently, both assertions assert of the same person that he is an author. There is but one fact, that a specific person is an author, which may, of course, be represented in different ways in different assertions. It possible that Mary only has a new representation of the same old materialistic facts

[19] James Frederick Ferrier, *Introduction to the Philosophy of Consciousness*, Pts. I –VII (1838–9), contained in *Lectures on Greek Philosophy and other Philosophical Remains*, ed. Sir Alexander Grant, Bt. and E. L. Lushington (Edinburgh and London, 1866), ii. 1–257; Thomas Nagel, 'What is it Like to Be a Bat?', *Philosophical Review*, 83 (1974), 1–22, and *The View from Nowhere* (New York, 1986); Frank Jackson, 'Epiphenomenal Qualities', pp. 127–36.

after she sees colour. But why does Mary have a different way of representing colour when she sees colours?

The answer to the question is contained in the notion of exemplarization and exemplaric representation. Exemplarization gives us knowledge of a sensation, of pain, for example, by means of unique exemplaric representation of the pain. The exemplaric representation of the pain uses the pain to represent itself among other pains and, as a result, it is a different representation from any other. In this way, exemplaric representation, whether of sensations of pain or colour, provides a new kind of knowledge. By analogy, notice that a person who knows that Mark Twain is an author, perhaps as a result of reading one of his novels, *Tom Sawyer*, for example, and noting the author of it, obtains new knowledge when he learns that Samuel Clemens is an author. This will be most apparent if the person learns the latter by being informed of the fact without learning that Mark Twain is Samuel Clemens. In that case, the person knows both that Mark Twain is an author and that Samuel Clemens is an author but, being ignorant of the identity of Mark Twain and Samuel Clemens, does not know that these two things that he knows are knowledge of the same fact, of one specific person being an author. Similarly, a person like monochromatic Mary will obtain new knowledge when she becomes conscious of colours for the first time. Consciousness of the new sensation of colour exemplarizes the sensation and gives her new knowledge of a fact by means of the exemplaric representation, the self-representation, of the sensation. Since she was not conscious of the sensation previously, she could know what the sensation was like in that way, that is, in terms of self-representation. The reason is that, not having had the sensation previously, she could not use the sensation to represent anything and especially not itself.

Exemplaric representation of a sensation yields knowledge which a person cannot obtain prior to consciousness of the sensation. The question that remains is whether this new knowledge is knowledge of some new fact beyond the facts that can be objectively or scientifically known. The example of Mark Twain and Samuel Clemens illustrates quite clearly that new knowledge does not entail knowledge of a new fact. Although exemplaric representation yields new knowledge for Mary, it does not follow that this new knowledge is knowledge of a new fact. It might just be a new way of knowing an old fact, one that she knew before under a different representation. However, the argument of the authors in question, from Ferrier to Jackson and Nagel, is that there is new knowledge of what the sensation is like, that is, of what quality the sensation has. Is that knowledge of a new kind of fact?

That would be an exciting but incorrect conclusion. Consciousness reveals a new way of representing facts, by exemplarization, and new knowledge generated by exemplaric representation, but such new knowledge is not proven thereby to reveal a new kind of fact. The new knowledge may be informative, of course, as the person who learns that Clemens is an author acquires new knowledge that is informative. But the fact that Clemens is an author is the same fact as that Twain is an author, and the fact that Mary's brother is conscious of the sensation of red may be the same fact as one described in Mary's complete knowledge of the physical world, including Mary's brother knowing what the sensation is like. For the latter knowledge is what he obtains by exemplarization. The new knowledge is fully explained by the new mode of representation, exemplaric representation, without appeal to a new kind of fact.

Does this theory of our looping knowledge of lucid content by exemplarization refute functional theories of content? Does it refute theories of wide and narrow content? It depends on whether such theories are articulated in a way that is consistent with the operation of looping, and, in fact, they may be articulated in a way consistent with such theories provided that there is some functional account of looping. I shall conclude with such an account, but it should not be construed as a defence of materialism.

Neural Activation: An Integrative Loop

I have argued for the importance of metamental ascent for
our knowledge of content and have tried to explain how it
works. In conclusion, I want to close the metamental loop
by coming back to the body and to neural activation. Have
the notions of metamental ascent and the metamental loop
so far removed us from neural activation that, if you follow
me where my conclusions draw us, you will have eliminated the possibility that the brain realizes such mental activity? In fact, I want to suggest there is a loop in neural
activation.

My argument is simple and mathematical, though left
here without neurological detail. The brain realizes the
mathematical model of aggregation considered above.
Neurophysiology recapitulates metamentality in a loop of
aggregation and weighted averaging.

These are the assumptions of my argument. It is necessary for the brain to average incoming input across neurons or neural groups. The brain must find the appropriate
set of weights for averaging. Neural activation realizes
weighted averaging. The weights are a set of numbers that
are non-negative and sum to 1. It is, moreover, important to
notice that the averaging of input is one standard model of
aggregating data, especially conflicting data, beyond the
applications that we have considered so far.

Probability Aggregations

The weights that are used for averaging are often the set of
prior probabilities of some set of disjoint and exhaustive alternative evidence statements. For example, when there are
various probabilities that might be assigned to a hypothesis, H, on the basis of various possible statements of evidence, $E1$, $E2$ and so forth to En, which are disjoint and
exhaustive, the probability of H is computed from the following fundamental theorem of Bayesian probability:

$$p(H) = p(H/E1)p(E1) + p(H/E2)p(E2) + \ldots + \\ p(H/En)p(En)$$

Another example is the Jeffrey formula for computing a new probability, p_N, of H as the result of assigning new probabilities to the evidence sets $E1$, $E2$, and so forth to En by appealing to the old conditional probabilities, p_O, of H on the evidence sets as follows:

$$p_N(H) = p_O(H/E1)p_N(E1) + p_O(H/E2)p_N(E2) + \ldots + p_O(H/En)p_N(En).$$ [20]

In these cases, the weights used to average the conditional probabilities are prior probabilities. As we noted earlier when considering consensus and integration concerning preferences, the weights used to average need not be probabilities, nor need the items averaged be probabilities. The weights may be evaluations of comparative trustworthiness of preferences of acceptances. The formula in a general form is, as we noted, as follows:

$$p_i^1(H) = p_1^0(H)w_{i1} + p_2^0(H)w_{i2} + \ldots + p_n^0(H)w_{in}.$$

This method of aggregation converges under the conditions specified earlier, when iterated.

The Vector Loop

Recall, before returning to the brain, that the process of aggregation is mathematically equivalent to finding a set of consensual weights from the diverse weights individuals assign to each other, or to perspectives within a single individual, to average the original probabilities or preferences. There is a unique set of weights, a fixed point vector, that yields the consensual weight for j that iterated averaging finds, namely, the set of consensual weights themselves. So the answer to the question of how to compute the consensual weights from the diverse weights assigned to j from diverse individuals or perspectives is contained in the following formula:

$$w_j = w_1w_{1j} + w_2w_{2j} + \ldots + w_jw_{jj} + \ldots w_nw_{nj}.$$

[20] Richard Jeffrey, *The Logic of Decision* (New York, 1965).

Inspection of the formula reveals the loop we noticed above. We use the consensual weight for j to compute to the weight for j, or, put another way, the consensual weights for members of the group or perspectives within the individual resulting from iterated aggregation are just those weights that yield themselves back when used to average the diverse weights assigned.

The Neural Loop

The foregoing model of weighted averaging with a loop may be applied to the brain. Suppose, as has been proposed, that neural activation is weighted averaging of neural input across the neurons. Start with the model of aggregation of probabilities or preferences but replace the initial probabilities or preferences with initial neural input to a neural unit within some connected group and consider the weights as modifying the level of activation of the neural units. Finally, suppose that integration of the initial neural input is accomplished by weighted averaging. The task of a neural network would be to find the appropriate set of weights by iterated averaging or some approximation thereof to achieve the integration of the input. The appropriate set of weights to produce integrative equilibrium, integrative weights, would be the fixed point vector, that is, the set of weights achieving equilibrium by yielding themselves back in the process of aggregation.

Thus, if there are weights w_{1j}, w_{2j}, and so forth to w_{nj}, that might be used to average input from neural unit j, then the formula above for averaging weights shows us that there is a fixed point vector containing an integrative weight for each neural unit. The fixed point vector, itself found by iterated averaging, finds an equilibrium integration of neural input. It is, moreover, precisely that unique vector that yields itself back, producing equilibrium in the process of aggregating neural input.

The foregoing proposal is, of course, highly schematic as well as speculative. It does, however, make an empirical prediction. The prediction is that the neural unit would need to receive considerable neural feedback or backward projection from other neural units in the network in order to find the integrative weights. Assuming that there is no localized centre in the brain for computing the fixed point vector, which surely there is not, the integrative weights must be found by feedback from neural units in the neural network altering the activation levels of the neural units. The interaction of the neural units can find the integrative weights or an approximation thereof without any localized centre for accomplishing this task only if there is considerable backward projection in the neurons in comparison to the forward projection of input activation. This appears to be the case. Backward projection could effect the integrative loop.

An activation loop is a possible neural realization of the loop of metamental activity. Of course, this is only a possibility, though I think it is a hypothesis worth exploring given the unique role of fixed point vectors in vector aggregation. The possibility shows that there is nothing in the notion of a metamental loop that could not be modelled within a vector activation theory of neural activity. I sought to mentalize the body with intentionality. I sought to metamentalize the mentalized body with knowledge and the metamental loop. I end with a conjecture about how to materialize the metamentalized body in neural vectors with a fixed point vector yielding itself.

Summary: Mind, Body, and the Loop

We have considered how the loop of self-representation of our mental life results from an internal loop of quotation and disquotation. The conversion of this operation to yield knowledge depends, however, on our understanding of the disquoted symbol, expression, or descriptor. Our knowledge of the content and the intentional object results from an internal loop of metamental quotation and disquotation based on the understanding of the symbol. The question is whether an account of the understanding of the disquoted symbol brings us back to some mysterious object that is understood—*meaning*. This does not seem to me the correct way to proceed. Suppose that there is some object which is the meaning of the symbol. To explain how we understand the symbol in terms of understanding the meaning of the symbol leaves us with the problem of explaining how we understand the meaning. Now someone might, of course, claim that our understanding of the meaning is immediate, but once immediacy ends the quest for explanation we may note that we might just as well have ended the quest earlier by claiming that the understanding of the symbol was immediate. There is no advantage in adding the mystery of understanding meaning to the mystery of understanding a symbol.

Understanding a symbol is understanding the role or function of the symbol, as many have insisted. Our knowledge of the content of the symbol may, of course, be expressed as our knowledge of the meaning of the symbol, but that knowledge, founded on the loop of self-representation, does not require the postulation of some special semantic object, a meaning, nor does the postulation of such an object assist in explaining how we understand the symbol.

What does explain our understanding of the symbol? It depends, of course, on the symbol. Take, however, a symbol such as a *pain*, used as a symbol of pain, or the word 'pain' used as a symbol to represent pains. Consider the word as symbol. Our understanding of the word is based on our understanding the function or role of the symbol as we connect it with other symbols and apply it to the external world. This understanding requires the resolution of conflict within individuals and between individuals. The resolution takes us into aggregation, as Adrienne Lehrer and I have proposed, which is something the neurons can do for us or we for them within a loop of consensual or integrative weights.[21]

---

[21] Adrienne Lehrer and Keith Lehrer, 'Fields, Networks and Vectors', in F. Palmer (ed.), *Grammar and Meaning* (New York, 1995), pp. 26–47.

Idealism and Materialism

The account of consciousness I have defended opposes eliminative materialism. I am equally opposed to eliminative idealism. The account of the internal loop of self-representation and exemplarization might appear to favour idealism. Our knowledge of the content of our thoughts and sentences results, I have proposed, from an internal loop of quotation and disquotation. Are we not, therefore, just representing our own descriptors in a loop of quotation and disquotation when we attempt to represent the material world? To conclude that would be to confuse our knowledge of the contents of our thoughts with the content known. The content becomes lucid as the result of the loop of quotation and disquotation, but the web of internal semantic and grammatical relations is connected to the external world by our application of our symbols to the external world as well as to our internal states.

The arguments we have given in defence of consciousness, based on the trustworthiness of our acceptance of the representations of consciousness, can be duplicated by replacing consciousness of the internal world with perception of the external world. We accept that we are trustworthy in our acceptance of one and the other. Preferring to be trustworthy, we accept that we think and feel and that we see and touch. The objects of the former acceptance are the mental states within us and the latter are the material states outside of us.

The modern age has been preoccupied with the mind–body problem. Some, beginning with their acceptance of the world within, have been led to deny the existence of matter, and others, beginning with their acceptance of the external world, have been led to deny the existence of mind. Both these kinds of philosophers have alleged that someone who affirms the existence of both will be led into intractable difficulties in explaining the relationship between them. I do not deny the perplexities, but the solution, which is not the object of the present work, is to be found within a loop that connects one with the other. When I reflect on my mind, I consider it to be the subject of my evaluation system, though not only that. When I reflect upon my brain, I consider it to be the subject of my evaluation system, though not only that. I think about my brain as best I can in my relative ignorance of it, and accept that it is the subject of my acceptances and preferences.

Is the mind nothing but the brain? The mind and brain are both subjects of acceptances and preferences, including acceptances and preferences concerning my trustworthiness. Am I my brain? Am I my body? I, who trust and am worthy of my trust, am mind and body. I am sure that my brain accepts that I have a mind and that my mind accepts that I have a brain. And I accept that I am trustworthy concerning what I accept about these matters. But what am I? I am, at least in part, a mentalized body. I am, at least in part, a materialized mind. There is a mathematical loop from the mentality of the body to the materiality of the mind, and the unity of the autonomous self is enclosed in the mathematical loop.

What am I? The mathematical loop of mind and body spirals autonomously outward in personal and social aggregation. I am the mathematical loop of trust and trustworthiness in the metamental ascent and descent of the mind and body in time and space. I may be more than that, but of that I am ignorant.

FOR FURTHER READING

On consciousness:

Boghossian, Paul, 'Content and Self-Knowledge', *Philosophical Topics*, 17 (1989), 5–26.

Brueckner, Anthony, 'Knowledge of Content and Knowledge of the World', *Philosophical Review*, 103 (1994), 327–43.

Burge, Tyler, 'Individualism and Self-Knowledge', *Journal of Philosophy*, 85 (1988), 649–63.

Dennett, Daniel C., *Consciousness Explained* (Boston, Mass.: Little, Brown & Company, 1991).

Pollock, John, *How to Build a Person: A Prolegomenon* (Cambridge, Mass.: MIT Press, 1989).

Rosenthal, David, 'Two Concepts of Consciousness', *Philosophical Studies*, 49 (1986), 329–59.

Shoemaker, Sydney, 'Lectures I, II and III: Self Knowledge and "Inner Sense"', *Philosophy and Phenomenological Research*, 54 (1994), 249–69, 271–90, 291–314.

On eliminative materialism:

Baker, Lynne Rudder, *Saving Belief* (Princeton, N.J.: Princeton University Press, 1987).

Churchland, Paul, 'Eliminative Materialism and the Propositional Attitudes', *Journal of Philosophy*, 78 (1981), 67–90.

—— 'Reduction, Qualia, and the Direct Introspection of Brain States', *Journal of Philosophy*, 82 (1985), 8–28.

Stich, Stephen P., *From Folk Psychology to Cognitive Science* (Cambridge, Mass.: MIT Press, 1983).

On mental representation:

Churchland, Patricia S., and Terence J. Sejnowski, *The Computational Brain* (Cambridge, Mass.: MIT Press, 1992).

Fodor, Jerry, *The Language of Thought* (New York: Thomas Y. Crowell, 1975).

—— *Psychosemantics* (Cambridge, Mass.: MIT Press, 1987).

Searle, John, *Intentionality: An Essay in the Philosophy of Mind* (New York: Cambridge University Press, 1983).

On higher-order evaluation:

Goldman, Alvin I., *Liaisons: Philosophy Meets the Cognitive and Social Sciences* (Cambridge, Mass.: Bradford Books, 1992).

Skyrms, Brian, 'Higher-Order Degrees of Belief', in D. H. Mellor (ed.), *Prospects for Pragmatism* (New York: Cambridge University Press, 1980).

Sosa, Ernest, *Knowledge in Perspective* (New York: Cambridge University Press, 1991).

8

The Mathematical Loop of Estavayer

I have followed the sequence of self-trust to the keystone loop of acceptance, preference, and reason for my being worthy of my trust concerning my acceptance, preference, and reason. Knowledge and wisdom are within the loop, and autonomy is at the centre of it. Remember the church at Estavayer with the arches supporting as they are supported by the keystone loop at the top. The arches are the arches of preference and acceptance, and they, together with the keystone loop of reason at the top, yield knowledge and wisdom.

I followed the sequence of self-trust beyond myself to the evaluation of others. I explored the structure of love and consensus resulting from my preferences for the preferences of others and my evaluation of them. Following self-trust to evaluation of the trustworthiness of others, I aggregate with them in my trust of myself and the other to enhance my trustworthiness in what I accept and prefer. In aggregation I incorporate the trustworthiness of others in my trustworthiness. The individual becomes a social aggregate at the same time as the individuals are aggregated to find the social consensus. Consensus is an aggregation of the weight we give to each other in evaluation and negotiation. The aggregation of individuals yields the social consensus within the consenting individuals. Each person aggregates making the resulting consensus her own.

There is a mathematical loop in consensus, for the consensual weights we seek are the ones we need to resolve the differences between us in the weights we assign to an individual. We need to find the consensual weights to aggregate the diverse weights we assign to each other. Individual aggregation discovers the consensual weights

by a kind of mathematical magic. A vicious circle becomes
a trustworthy loop as we aggregate in our evaluation and
negotiation with others. As we aggregate within we find
the same mathematical loop of trustworthiness within. The
aggregation within the neural assemblies of the brain
would employ the same mathematical magic we find in
personal and social consensus. There is a mathematical
keystone loop supporting aggregation as aggregation supports it, discovering the consensual loop turning conflict
into consensus.

The keystone loop at Estavayer can, with an increase of
arches, connect and integrate without limit. From the perspective of a given arch, the other arches may seem prob-
lematically rife with the potential for conflict. But the
mathematical loop holds them together, supported by
them as it supports them. The most important feature of
the loop becomes clearer as we think of the arches multi-
plying to fill the space between them. For then it becomes
clear that keystone loop is only a part of the arches and not
anything separate from them. Within the mathematical
loop we find the unity of perspectives, the unity of individual and society, of mind and body. In consciousness we
find a loop of metamental ascent and objective descent to
yield our knowledge of the content of thought and, hence,
of acceptance and preference.

You might be inclined to ask what the loop is. Is it preference or acceptance? Is it individual or social? Is it mind or
body? Is it abstract or concrete? The answer, of course, is
that it is an actualized mathematical structure that realizes
quantity and quality, individual and society, mind and
body. Reality is mathematical as the Pythagoreans affirmed
and many a physicist will insist when asked whether reality is made of waves or corpuscles. You can only understand this answer from within the loop. The fundamental
answer is the mathematical loop. If you do not understand,
return to the beginning, read, evaluate and aggregate. You
will find the answer within the loop.

BIBLIOGRAPHY

Alston, William P., 'Epistemic Circularity', *Philosophy and Pheno-menological Research*, 47 (1986), 1–30.

—— 'Thomas Reid on Epistemic Principles', *History of Philosophy Quarterly*, 2 (1985), 435–52.

—— 'Two Types of Foundationalism', *Journal of Philosophy*, 73 (1976), 165–85.

Audi, Robert, *Belief, Justification and Knowledge* (Belmont, Calif.: Wadsworth, 1988).

Baccarini, Elvio, 'Rational Consensus and Coherence Methods in Ethics', *Grazer Philosophische Studien*, 40 (1991), 151–9.

Baier, Annette, 'Trust', in Grethe Peterson (ed.), *The Tanner Lectures on Human Values* (Salt Lake City, Utah: University of Utah Press, 1992).

Baigrie, Brian, and J. Hattiangadi, 'On Consensus and Stability in Science', *British Journal for the Philosophy of Science*, 43 (1992), 435–58.

Baird, Davis, 'Lehrer–Wagner Consensual Probabilities do not Adequately Summarize the Available Information', *Synthese*, 62 (1985), 47–62.

Baker, Lynne Rudder, *Saving Belief* (Princeton, N.J.: Princeton University Press, 1987).

Bartlett, Steven (ed.), *Reflexivity: A Source-Book in Self-Reference* (New York: Elsevier Science, 1992).

Bender, John W. (ed.), *The Current State of the Coherence Theory* (Boston, Mass., and Dordrecht: Kluwer Academic Publishers, 1989).

Berger, R. L., 'A Necessary and Sufficient Condition for Reaching a Consensus by De Groot's Method', *Journal of the American Statistical Association*, 76 (1981), 415–18.

Black, Max, 'Self-Supporting Inductive Arguments', *Journal of Philosophy*, 55 (1958), 718–25.

Boghossian, Paul, 'Content and Self-Knowledge', *Philosophical Topics*, 17 (1989), 5–26.

BonJour, Laurence, *The Structure of Empirical Knowledge* (Cambridge, Mass.: Harvard University Press, 1985).

Braaten, Jane, 'Rational Consensual Procedure: Argumentation or Weighted Averaging', *Synthese*, 71 (1987), 347–53.

Brueckner, Anthony, 'Knowledge of Content and Knowledge of the World', *Philosophical Review*, 103 (1994), 327–43.

Burge, Tyler, 'Individualism and Self-Knowledge', *Journal of Philosophy*, 85 (1988), 649–63.

Chisholm, Roderick, *Theory of Knowledge*, 3rd edn. (Englewood Cliffs, N.J.: Prentice-Hall, 1989).

—— 'The Status of Epistemic Principles', *Nous*, 24 (1990), 209–15.

Christiano, Thomas, 'Freedom, Consensus, and Equality in Collective Decision Making', *Ethics*, 101 (1990), 151–81 .

Churchland, Patricia S., and Terence J. Sejnowski, *The Computational Brain* (Cambridge, Mass.: MIT Press, 1992).

Churchland, Paul, 'Eliminative Materialism and the Propositional Attitudes', *Journal of Philosophy*, 78 (1981), 67–90.

—— 'Reduction, Qualia, and the Direct Introspection of Brain States', *Journal of Philosophy*, 82 (1985), 8–28.

Cohen, Jonathan L., *The Probable and the Provable* (Oxford: Clarendon Press, 1977).

Cohen, Stewart, 'Justification and Truth', *Philosophical Studies*, 46 (1984), 279–95.

Dennett, Daniel C., *Consciousness Explained* (Boston: Little, Brown & Company, 1991).

—— *Elbow Room: The Varieties of Free Will Worth Wanting* (Cambridge, Mass.: MIT Press, 1984).

De Groot, M. H., 'Reaching a Consensus', *Journal of the American Statistical Association*, 69 (1974), 118–212.

De Sousa, Ronald, *The Rationality of Emotion* (Cambridge, Mass.: MIT Press, 1987).

Dretske, Fred, 'Conscious Experience', *Mind*, 102 (1993), 263–83.

—— *Knowledge and the Flow of Information* (Cambridge, Mass.: MIT Press, 1981).

Ekstrom, Laura Waddell, 'A Coherence Theory of Autonomy', *Philosophy and Phenomenological Research*, 53 (1993), 599–616.

Falvey, Kevin, and Joseph Owens, 'Externalism, Self-Knowledge, and Skepticism', *Philosophical Review*, 103 (1994), 107–37.

Feigl, Herbert, 'On the Vindication of Induction', *Philosophy of Science*, 28 (1961), 212–16.

Ferrier, James Frederick, *Introduction to the Philosophy of Consciousness*, Pts. i–vii, (1838–9), contained in *Lectures on Greek Philosophy and other Philosophical Remains*, vol. ii, ed. by Sir Alexander

Grant, Bt. and E. L. Lushington (Edinburgh and London: William Blackwood & Sons, 1866).

Fodor, Jerry, 'Cognitive Science and the Twin-Earth Problem', *Notre Dame Journal of Formal Logic*, 23 (1982), 98–118.

—— *The Language of Thought* (New York: Thomas Y. Crowell, 1975).

—— *Psychosemantics* (Cambridge, Mass.: MIT Press, 1987).

Foley, Richard, *A Theory of Epistemic Rationality* (Cambridge, Mass.: Harvard University Press, 1987).

—— 'What am I to Believe?', in Steven Wagner and Richard Warner (eds.), *Naturalism: A Critical Appraisal* (Notre Dame, Ind.: University of Notre Dame Press, 1993).

Forrest, Peter, 'The Lehrer–Wagner Theory of Consensus and the Zero Weight Problem', *Synthese*, 62 (1985), 75–8.

Frankfurt, Harry, 'Freedom of the Will and the Concept of a Person', *Journal of Philosophy*, 68 (1971), 5–20.

French, Peter A., Theodore E. Uehling, and Howard K. Wettstein (eds.), *Midwest Studies in Philosophy*, 10 (Minneapolis, Minn.: University of Minnesota Press, 1986).

Gettier, Edmund Jr., 'Is Justified True Belief Knowledge?', *Analysis*, 23 (1963), 121 –3.

Gibbard, Allan, *Wise Choices, Apt Feelings* (Cambridge, Mass., and Oxford: Harvard University Press and Clarendon Press, 1990).

Goldman, Alvin I., 'Consciousness, Folk Psychology, and Cognitive Science', *Consciousness and Cognition*, 2 (1993), 364–82.

—— *Epistemology and Cognition* (Cambridge, Mass.: Harvard University Press, 1986).

—— *Liaisons: Philosophy Meets the Cognitive and Social Sciences* (Cambridge, Mass.: Bradford Books, 1992).

—— 'The Psychology of Folk Psychology', *Behavioral and Brain Sciences*, 16 (1993), 15–28.

Goodman, Nelson, *Languages of Art* (Indianapolis, Ind.: Bobbs-Merrill Publishing Co., 1968).

Gopnik, Alison, 'How we Know our Minds: The Illusion of First-Person Knowledge of Intentionality', *Behavioral and Brain Sciences*, 16 (1993), 1–14.

Grofman, Bernard, and Carole Uhlaner, 'Metapreferences and the Reasons for Stability in Social Choice', *Theory and Decision*, 19 (1985), 31–50.

Gutman, Amy, and Dennis Thompson, 'Moral Conflict and Political Consensus', *Ethics*, 101 (1990), 64–88.

Hardwig, John, 'The Role of Trust in Knowledge', *Journal of Philosophy*, 88 (1991), 693–708.

Harman, Gilbert, *Change in View* (Cambridge, Mass.: MIT Press, 1986).

Heil, John, 'Believing Reasonably', *Nous*, 26 (1992), 47–62.

—— *The Nature of True Minds* (New York: Cambridge University Press, 1992).

Hofstadter, Douglas, *Gödel, Escher, Bach: An Eternal Golden Braid* (New York: Basic Books, 1979).

Holton, Richard, 'Deciding to Trust, Coming to Believe', *Australasian Journal of Philosophy*, 72 (1994), 63-76.

Horgan, Terence, 'From Supervenience to Superdupervenience: Meeting the Demands of a Material World', *Mind*, 102 (1993), 555–86.

Jackson, Frank, 'Epiphenomenal Qualities', *Philosophical Quarterly*, 32 (1982), 127–36.

Jeffrey, Richard, *The Logic of Decision* (New York: McGraw-Hill, 1965).

—— 'Preferences among Preferences', *Journal of Philosophy*, 71 (1974), 377–91 .

Kagan, Shelly, *The Limits of Morality* (Oxford: Clarendon Press, 1989).

Kant, Immanuel, *Foundations of the Metaphysics of Morals* (1785), 1st edn. trans. and intro. by Lewis White Beck (Indianapolis, Ind.: Bobbs-Merrill Publishing Co., 1975).

Kim, Jaegwon, 'Concepts of Supervenience', *Philosophy and Phenomenological Research*, 45 (1984), 153–76.

—— *Supervenience and Mind* (New York: Cambridge University Press, 1993).

Klagge, James, 'Supervenience: Ontological and Ascriptive', *Australasian Journal of Philosophy*, 66 (1988), 461–70.

Klein, Peter, *Certainty: A Refutation of Scepticism* (Minneapolis, Minn.: University of Minnesota Press, 1981).

Kordig, Carl, 'Self-Reference and Philosophy', *American Philosophical Quarterly*, 20 (1983), 207–16.

Kvanvig, Jonathan, 'Is There an "Us" in "Justification"?', *Synthese*, 62 (1985), 63–74.

Lamb, Roger (ed.), *Love Analyzed* (Boulder, Colo.: Westview Press, 1996).

Lehrer, Adrienne, *Wine and Conversation* (Bloomington, Ind.: Indiana University Press, 1983).

—— and Keith Lehrer, 'Fields, Networks and Vectors', in F. Palmer (ed.), *Grammar and Meaning* (New York: Cambridge University Press, 1995), 26–47.

Lehrer, Keith, 'Coherence and the Racehorse Paradox', in Peter A. French *et al.* (eds.), *Midwest Studies in Philosophy*, 5 (1980), 183–92.

—— 'Coherence, Consensus and Language', *Linguistics and Philosophy*, 7 (1984), 43–56.

—— 'Denying Deception: A Reply to Terry Price', *Philosophical Studies*, 74 (1994), 283–90.

—— *Metamind* (Oxford: Clarendon Press, 1990).

—— 'Metamind, Autonomy and Materialism', *Grazer Philosophische Studien*, 40 (1991), 1–11 .

—— 'Personal and Social Knowledge', *Synthese*, 73 (1987), 87–108.

—— *Theory of Knowledge* (Boulder, Colo., and London: Westview Press and Routledge, 1990).

—— *Thomas Reid* (New York: Routledge, 1989).

—— Jeannie Lum, Beverly Slichta, and Nicholas Smith (eds.), *Knowledge, Teaching, and Wisdom* (Boston, Mass.: Kluwer Academic Publishers, 1996).

—— and Carl Wagner, 'Intransitive Indifference: The Semi-Order Problem', *Synthese*, 65 (1985), 249–56.

—— —— *Rational Consensus in Science and Society* (Dordecht: Reidel, 1981).

Levi, Isaac, 'Consensus as Shared Agreement and Outcome of Inquiry', *Synthese*, 62 (1985), 3–12.

Loewer, Barry (ed.), *Consensus,* a special issue of *Synthese,* 62 (1985).

—— and Robert Laddaga, 'Destroying the Consensus', *Synthese*, 62 (1985), 79–96.

Luce, Duncan, 'Semi-Orders and a Theory of Utility Discrimination', *Econometrica*, 24 (1956), 178–91.

Lycan, William G., *Judgement and Justification* (New York: Cambridge University Press, 1988).

MacIntosh, Duncan, 'Preference Revision and the Paradoxes of Instrumental Rationality', *Canadian Journal of Philosophy*, 22 (1992), 503–29.

Mele, Alfred, 'Akrasia, Self-Control, and Second-Order Desires', *Nous*, 26 (1992), 281–302.

—— 'Incontinent Believing', *Philosophical Quarterly*, 36 (1986), 212–22.

Moser, Paul K., *Knowledge and Evidence* (New York: Cambridge University Press, 1989).

Nagel, Thomas, 'Sexual Perversion', *Journal of Philosophy* 65 (1969), 5–17.

—— *The View from Nowhere* (New York: Oxford University Press, 1986).

—— 'What is it Like to Be a Bat?' *Philosophical Review*, 83 (1974), 1–22.

Neely, Wright, 'Freedom and Desire', *Philosophical Review*, 83 (1974), 32–54.

Nisbett, Richard, and Lee Ross, *Human Inference: Strategies and Shortcomings of Social Judgment* (Englewood Cliffs, N.J.: Prentice-Hall, 1980).

Nozick, Robert, *Philosophical Explanations* (Cambridge, Mass.: Harvard University Press, 1981).

Nurmi, Hannu, 'Some Properties of the Lehrer–Wagner Method for Reaching Rational Consensus', *Synthese*, 62 (1985), 13–24.

Nussbaum, Martha, *Love's Knowledge* (New York: Oxford University Press, 1990).

Plantinga, Alvin, *Warrant and Proper Function* (New York: Oxford University Press, 1993).

Pollock, John, *Contemporary Theories of Knowledge* (Totowa, N.J.: Rowman & Littlefield, 1986).

—— *How to Build a Person: A Prolegomenon* (Cambridge, Mass.: MIT Press, 1989).

Price, Terry L., 'Counterexamples and Prophylactics', *Philosophical Studies*, 74 (1994), 273–82.

Putnam, Hilary, *Mind, Language, and Reality* (New York: Cambridge University Press, 1975).

Reichenbach, Hans, 'On the Justification of Induction', *Journal of Philosophy*, 37 (1940), 97–103.

Reid, Thomas, *Essays on the Active Powers of Man* (Edinburgh, 1785).

—— *Essays on the Intellectual Powers of Man* (Edinburgh, 1785).

—— *The Works of Thomas Reid, D.D.*, 8th edn., ed. by Sir William Hamilton (Edinburgh: James Thin, 1895).

Rescher, Nicholas, *Pluralism: Against the Demand for Consensus* (Oxford: Clarendon Press, 1993).

Rorty, Amélie Oksenberg, 'The Historicity of Psychological Attitudes', in Peter A. French, Theodore E. Uehling, and Howard K. Wettstein (eds.), *Midwest Studies in Philosophy*, 10 (1986), 399–412.

Rosenthal, David, 'Thinking that one Thinks', in Martin Davies (ed.), *Consciousness: Psychological and Philosophical Essays* (Oxford: Blackwell, 1993).

—— 'Two Concepts of Consciousness', *Philosophical Studies*, 49 (1986), 329–59.

Roth, Michael, and Glenn Ross, *Doubting: Contemporary Perspectives on Skepticism* (Boston, Mass.: Kluwer Academic Publishers, 1992).

Sartre, Jean-Paul, *Being and Nothingness*, trans. Hazel E. Barnes (New York: Philosophical Library, 1956).

Sayre-McCord, Geoffrey (ed.), *Essays on Moral Realism* (Ithaca, N.Y.: Cornell University Press, 1988).

Schmitt, Frederick, 'Consensus, Respect, and Weighted Averaging', *Synthese*, 62 (1985), 25–46.

Searle, John, *Intentionality: An Essay in the Philosophy of Mind* (New York: Cambridge University Press, 1983).

Sellars, Wilfrid, *Science, Perception and Reality* (New York: Humanities Press, 1963).

Shafir, E., and A. Tversky, 'Thinking through Uncertainty: Nonconsequential Reasoning and Choice', *Cognitive Psychology*, 24 (1992), 449–74.

Shoemaker, Sydney, 'Lectures I, II and III: Self Knowledge and "Inner Sense"', *Philosophy and Phenomenological Research*, 54 (1994), 249–69, 271–90, 291–314.

Skyrms, Brian, 'Higher-Order Degrees of Belief', in D. H. Mellor (ed.), *Prospects for Pragmatism* (New York: Cambridge University Press, 1980).

Sosa, Ernest, *Knowledge in Perspective* (New York: Cambridge University Press, 1991).

Stich, Stephen P., *From Folk Psychology to Cognitive Science* (Cambridge, Mass.: MIT Press, 1983).

Suber, Peter, 'A Bibliography of Works on Reflexivity', in Peter Suber (ed.), *Self-Reference* (Dordrecht: Nijhoff, 1987).

Swain, Marshall, *Reasons and Knowledge* (Ithaca, N.Y.: Cornell University Press, 1981).

Swanton, Christine, *Freedom: A Coherence Theory* (Indianapolis, Ind.: Hackett Publishing Co., 1992).

Thalberg, I., 'Hierarchical Analyses of Unfree Action', *Canadian Journal of Philosophy*, 8 (1978), 211–26.

Van Cleve, James, 'Epistemic Supervenience and the Circle of Belief', *The Monist*, 68 (1985), 90–104.

Van Cleve, James (cont.)

—— 'Foundationalism, Epistemic Principles and the Cartesian Circle', *Philosophical Review*, 88 (1979), 55–91.

Wagner, Carl, 'On the Formal Properties of Weighted Averaging as a Method of Aggregation', *Synthese*, 62 (1985), 97–108.

Watson, Gary, 'Free Agency', *Journal of Philosophy*, 72 (1975), 205–20.

Zimmerman, David, 'Hierarchical Motivation and Freedom of the Will', *Pacific Philosophical Quarterly*, 62 (1981), 354–68.

INDEX

Note: a page reference accompanied by an 's' (e.g. Alston 76s) denotes an author listing in a supplementary reading section. Where there are multiple listings for that author on that page, such references may be followed by a number in parentheses (e.g. Alston 23s (2)), that denotes the number of listings on that page.